# Communicating
# TERROR

# Communicating TERROR

## The Rhetorical Dimensions of Terrorism

# Joseph S. Tuman
## San Francisco State University

**SAGE Publications**
*International Educational and Professional Publisher*
Thousand Oaks ■ London ■ New Delhi

*For information:*

Sage Publications, Inc.
2455 Teller Road
Thousand Oaks, California 91320
E-mail: order@sagepub.com

Sage Publications Ltd.
6 Bonhill Street
London EC2A 4PU
United Kingdom

Sage Publications India Pvt. Ltd.
B-42 Panchsheel Enclave
Post Box 4109
New Delhi 110017 India

Printed in the United States of America

*Library of Congress Cataloging-in-Publication Data*

Tuman, Joseph S.
Communicating terror: The rhetorical dimensions of terrorism / by Joseph S. Tuman.
   p. cm.
Includes bibliographical references and index.
ISBN 0-7619-2765-4 (Cloth) — ISBN 0-7619-2766-2 (Paper)
   1. Terrorism. 2. Terrorism and mass media. I. Title.
HV6431.T845 2003
303.6′25—dc21

                            2003004914

03   04   10   9   8   7   6   5   4   3   2   1

| | |
|---|---|
| *Acquiring Editor:* | Todd R. Armstrong |
| *Editorial Assistant:* | Heather Scafidi |
| *Production Editor:* | Diana E. Axelsen |
| *Copy Editor:* | Elisabeth Magnus |
| *Typesetter:* | C&M Digitals (P) Ltd. |
| *Indexer:* | Judy Hunt |
| *Cover Designer:* | Ravi Balasuriya/Michelle Lee |

# Contents

# Preface

On the morning of September 12, 2001, I was set to teach a class in political communications at San Francisco State University in California. As I came to class at the university, I found a group of students who were not in any mood to hear me discuss tactics and strategy for presidential debates. I cannot say that I felt any differently. It was the last thing on my mind at that time. Less than 24 hours before, for me and for every one of my students, our world as we knew it had changed. Our homeland—a place within which we feel comfort and security—had been attacked, and thousands of people—other Americans like us—had been killed. Murdered!

Like many people the day before, I too had remained glued to my television set, monitoring events in New York, Washington, and, to a lesser degree, Pennsylvania. I felt a sense of urgency about what was happening that was greater than almost any other I could recall in my life—except perhaps for the assassination of President Kennedy or the later assassinations of Dr. Martin Luther King, Jr., and Robert Kennedy. September 11, for me, had that kind of gravitas.

There was a similar mood among the students in my political communications class on this next morning, although they had considerable difficulty articulating what made them so uneasy. Perhaps like some of the readers of this book, these students were young, the average age being about 20 years old. In their lifetimes, they had witnessed political turmoil in elections (many had carefully followed the presidential election and the controversy over the Florida returns), a presidential impeachment, and even natural disasters like the Loma Prieta earthquake in the San Francisco Bay Area. Each of these events, like September 11, had taken center stage with maximum media attention. All of these students had their own attentiveness focused by that media scrutiny, as well as by personal involvement (e.g., many had lived in the earthquake zone). They had observed turmoil from afar and had physically lived through disaster up close.

In short, they understood what a moment of gravitas might entail—but somehow, on September 12, they still found the events of the preceding day different and perplexing. I saw that in their expressions on that morning and almost immediately abandoned my lecture. We spent 2 hours talking about what had happened. I asked them how they felt about the events of the previous day. How had these events changed their perspective of life here?

Of course, all of us know more about 9/11 today than we did the day after—but even at that time, some interesting answers to my questions emerged. For many students, what was troubling about the attacks was that they occurred *here* and not somewhere else. By *here,* they meant the United States. I asked: Did that mean they would have been less affected if the events had occurred in another country—like Japan or Russia or India? At the time, no one was willing to make that kind of claim—although a few students did clarify their original position, explaining that they had always felt safe and secure here. Acts of conventional war, or even acts of terrorism, were for the most part regrettable events that occurred somewhere else—and *to* somebody else.

Was there anything specific about the nature (e.g., spectacular, large-scale explosions, the demolition of the World Trade Center, fleeing victims) of the attacks that affected the students? Several students used the following words to describe their sense of the attacks—and their word choice was startling. Many said, "I felt like I was watching a movie. Things aren't supposed to happen like this in real life. This didn't seem real." One student added here that "all those television news outlets (and that was all of them) that decided to broadcast the story kept showing the *same* video over and over and over again. You know the one." With her last words, many students in class nodded appreciatively. Even I knew she was describing the video that showed the jets actually hitting the buildings and, later, the buildings collapsing.

Many students also indicated that they had experienced difficulty going on with a normal routine for the rest of their day on the eleventh—and several added that they had had trouble sleeping that night. "I know it sounds crazy," one student pointed out. "After all, this happened on the other side of the country. But it still felt like it was happening here. I felt just as vulnerable."

Perhaps you had a similar experience with 9/11? Maybe you felt as if what had happened in New York and Pennsylvania and Washington had actually happened to you where you live? There was a communal sense of loss on that day—as well as a collective sense of terror and fear. But how real was the loss? In our little world, in a classroom on the other side of the country, we were as far removed from New York and Pennsylvania and Washington as one could be, unless one resided in Hawaii or Alaska. In retrospect, how real was the risk and the threat—and how much of it was constructed by us and for us?

This is not in any way to diminish the very real threat of what we call terrorism or its potential for incurring great violence in our society; after all, several thousand people lost their lives on September 11 in all three locations. Nevertheless, how is it that a tragedy still so far removed from our own situation becomes a part of our perceived reality?

This was the question that nagged at me as I listened to the fears of my students—and later as I interviewed other individuals in the preparation of this book. For example, Rosemary B., an American expatriate and mother of twins, now living in London, had just arrived in Great Britain via San Francisco when the attacks occurred. On reaching her apartment, she immediately went to the television set and tracked events in the United States by CNN and the BBC. In her own words: "I was terrified and upset. This was different from anything I could remember. And at my last job—as a lawyer—I knew people who worked at the World Trade Center. . . . So I tried calling home, to reach my family in California, but their lines were absolutely jammed, which only heightened my sense of anxiety. When I finally did reach my mom, she was watching things on TV, too. And in the background I could hear my father complaining, 'This is worse than Pearl Harbor!'"

Rosemary's husband, Edward, also an American expatriate, found himself alarmed by the events of September 11 and by how much it affected his wife and family. One of his twins—a 4-year-old—complained of having nightmares about planes crashing into her bedroom window. Edward quickly tired of the same video footage on the news reports, depicting the jets crashing into the towers. "They wouldn't stop showing that," he shared, "and finally I had to ask Rosemary to shut it off."

Again, for people so far from home, the threat of this violence and the impact of the attacks was very real, even if separated by the distance of the Atlantic Ocean. Interestingly, Rosemary added: "Over several days, I got tired of hearing and seeing news information told by broadcasters who weren't familiar to me. I wanted news people I knew. Peter Jennings, Dan Rather, someone like that. Someone American. Someone who gets it, who understood what I was feeling. It made the news harder to take in, being told by someone else."

Like the comments of my students in the political communications class, the statements of both Rosemary and her husband reinforced the powerful role of television in this tragedy. Television was the medium of information for both Rosemary and her parents, and it primed and provoked their reactions when they spoke on the phone. The same was true of this medium's role in the way her husband and she absorbed this information, as well as how it was shared with her children. In fact, so powerful and dominant was the role television played that Rosemary actually longed for a more familiar face and voice on the television screen when watching to learn more about the attacks. There is comfort in the familiar.

But the *role of television* does not tell the whole story here. Television is but one form of *mass media,* which can be categorized into *news media* and *entertainment media,* as well as into *broadcast media* and *print media.* Unquestionably, news media in the forms of both broadcast and print news media helped construct public perceptions of the events on September 11 during and after the attacks. But equally so, entertainment media (which can also include television, cinema, and entertainment books) had already helped to precondition these same perceptions for many years—especially in the ways terrorism and terrorists had been portrayed in cinema from Hollywood. Additionally, as the above narratives suggest, there was *discourse* about these attacks that primed and provoked people's reactions. That discourse—the discussions, conversations, and processing and internalizing of information—was conducted within groups and between people around the country, if not the world.

The discourse was also primed by the rhetoric of world leaders—especially those here in the United States, and others in the Middle East—in response to the attacks, whether in the form of speeches (either in text or in sound-bite form) by individuals such as President George W. Bush or taped statements from Osama bin Laden and others in Afghanistan.

My students', Rosemary's, and others' perceptions of the reality and the threat of terrorist violence on that day and for months afterwards were, to a great deal, constructed. In truth, none of us was at more risk of physical violence from terrorism on September 12 than we had been on September 10. There had been attacks on U.S. military assets and embassy posts in the preceding years—all of which were known to the public. The World Trade Center itself had been bombed 8 years before the attack of 9/11. There had also been no shortage of examples of what might be called domestic terrorism—such as the Oklahoma City bombing—that were well-known and reported. So what had changed?

The answer to that question is the subject of this book and deals with the aforementioned *constructing* of terrorism. In the chapters that follow, we will examine how terrorism is most fundamentally understood as a communication process with rhetorical dimensions. We will explore how those dimensions are developed and intertwined in what I will call *rhetorical strands*—places where public discourse affects and is affected by defining and labeling of terror, the symbolic meaning of terrorism, public oratory about terror, and the interaction of terrorism and mass media.

No work like this can result without the very significant contributions of other people. Consequently, I would like to offer my thanks to Douglas Fraleigh at California State University, Fresno; Nicholas Burnett at California State University, Sacramento; and Gregory Payne at Emerson College, for valuable insights and suggestions in reviewing the complete manuscript. I also thank Hank Plante of KPIX-CBS for asking questions that starting me thinking about this topic, and Alicia Dlugosh of KTVU-Fox for her kind assistance with research. Additional thanks are offered to Patricia Palmerton at Hamline University, Randall Rogan at Wake Forest University, Ramona Rush at the University of Kentucky, Mehdi Semati at Eastern Illinois University, and Richard Vatz at Towson University for kindly reviewing early drafts of the book and providing valuable feedback about the project, as well as to Todd Armstrong, Alison Mudditt, and Heather Scafidi at Sage Publications for their assistance in shepherding this project from a conversation in my office to the finished product, and to my good friend Laurel for her advice about when to write and when to reflect.

Final thanks must go to my children, Helen and Nathaniel, who kindly gave up parts of their summer to help their father with research into a subject I wish they never had to know about, as well as to my loving wife, Kirsten, who graciously looked the other way as I lugged a laptop around Burgundy working on this project when we were supposed to be enjoying a vacation to the wine country. A wise person once told me that a writer's family and loved ones can be his or her best resource.

# Introduction

Humans perceive events through the prism of their own worldview and life experience as these are in turn affected by culture (a loaded, often abused term), education, age, national origin, philosophical or religious underpinnings (or the absence thereof), and the like. All of us have shared the experience of witnessing an event and then reacting with absolute surprise to hear others who had also been present describe that event in totally different ways that were at times even contradictory to our own perception. For example, two partners in a relationship may perceive very differently an issue that divides them, or partisan baseball fans may recall bitterly how they saw a pitch the umpire called as a third strike. In such instances, however, differences in perception will seldom be categorized with academic labels like *worldview* or *life experience*; more often they will be described as the product of one's *agenda*. In this way, it is suggested that we construct our perceptions of events according to the personal *agenda* it serves for us. Although this term is overly generalized and is not as useful as a more specific descriptor of human biases and motivations, it may still serve our purposes when we focus on the controversial topic that serves as the subject of this book: terrorism.

What is terrorism? Where does the word come from, and how is it used? For how long has it been a part of our vocabulary? How has it changed throughout the centuries? You may be surprised to know the answers. The word has origins and meanings in many cultures. Those who have studied it in the past four decades have often given contradictory definitions of the word that in turn have fueled controversy about how serious a problem it presents, whatever moral legitimacy it claims or lacks, and how nations and the global community should respond to it. We will address these definitions more fully in the next two chapters. For the time being, it serves to note that the existence of so many definitions raises questions about whose interests or agendas are being served by doing the defining. All of us (myself included) are the products of life experience that informs our own worldview and influences the way we may approach this topic. The reader is cautioned, therefore, to exhibit at least a very healthy curiosity about what any writer asserts about terrorism. In that sense, I encourage you to employ your best critical thinking skills when approaching this topic and those who write about it.

And lest I be accused of preaching one thing and practicing another, let me also encourage the reader to start that critical thinking with me. Who am I? What, if any, is my agenda? Academically, my background is in political science and law—a seemingly good combination for this subject. My research and teaching interests, however, are in communication studies (political and legal communications). Although I am well versed in this subject matter, I do not intend to offer you a book that merely restates much of the very good work that has been authored by historians, sociologists, political scientists, criminologists, and international relations experts. Thus, I am not interested in restating historical debates about terrorism as a moral response to imperialism or colonialism or semantic discussion about whether terrorism and guerrilla actions are distinct. I will not attempt psychological profiling of terrorists, nor will I attempt to resolve age-old international disputes, such as those in Northern Ireland or in the Middle East. That ground has already been covered, and by scholars, thinkers, and politicians far better equipped to address the issues. Instead, in this book, I wish to address terrorism by playing to my own particular interests, strengths, and background in political and legal communications. I will approach this subject by delving into its communicative properties and rhetorical dimensions.

To be clear, in the coming chapters I will argue that the meaning of terrorism is socially constructed. By that I mean that what we call terrorism is different and distinct from murder, assault, arson, destruction of property, or the threat of the same, primarily because the impact of terrorist violence and destruction reaches more than the immediate targeted victims. Although this in no way diminishes the pain and suffering of those immediate victims of terror, it does suggest that this violence and destruction becomes terrorism primarily because of its additional capacity to communicate message and meaning to a larger set of audiences.

In a later chapter, I offer a new definition of terrorism chiefly as a process of communication between terrorists and multiple target audiences. I will further argue that the way all audiences engage in discourse about terrorism is the manner by which we negotiate the meaning of terrorism. At this level, terrorism may also be seen as rhetorical, for there are several ways that rhetoric envelops the communication process by which we negotiate the meaning of this subject. These rhetorical strands form the rest of the book. In Chapter 3, we will re-examine the process of defining terrorism as the product of rhetorical choice, distinguishing between defining and labeling, and examining how the act of definition involves empowerment and marginalization.

In Chapter 4, we consider a different rhetorical strand by examining how terrorist violence and destruction may be seen as symbolic and once more how the meaning of these symbols is negotiated by and between different target audiences. Here I will review symbolism in terror by considering specific acts of violence, means and tools of terror, and targets of terrorism.

In Chapter 5, we will review how public rhetoric about terrorism is constructed and in what ways it may affect discourse between targeted audiences. Although there are many examples of public pronouncements by world leaders to consider here, in this chapter I focus on the American presidency and, for reasons of space and economy, on two influential speeches of President George W. Bush concerning September 11. Several tools for critically examining these types of public oratory will be offered as a means to evaluate and understand how this rhetoric works and why it affects social construction of terrorism.

In Chapter 6, I consider a final rhetorical strand—terrorism and mass media—to explore how mediated imagery also affects and sometimes preconditions our negotiation of the meaning of terrorism. Here we examine mass media as both entertainment and news, as broadcast and print, and assess the symbiotic relationship between terrorism and each of these forms of media.

The end product of this should be a fully developed set of tools with which to understand and see terrorism differently from before. As suggested above, I do not presume that any particular solution to this problem can be immediately found in this approach, although I do believe that giving a different set of tools to understand terrorism is an important first step to developing a response and comprehending why and how it has the capacity to affect us so deeply.

This explains my agenda and intentions in this work. It is also important for the reader—you—to consider your own life experience and worldview when approaching terrorism. What is your agenda here? This will be one of the first new books on this subject to emerge post–September 11. Indeed, the tragedy and shock of 9/11 may be the primary reason you are studying this topic in the first place. Consequently, there are three notions I want you to consider in approaching this writing.

First, be aware that this book will include analysis of 9/11 as part of a larger perspective of terrorism and rhetoric but that it is not just a book about 9/11. Indeed, it may still be too close in time to that event for any kind of comprehensive understanding of it or perspective on it. In fact, as I will shortly describe, this book will cover a great many more examples of rhetoric and terror in the United States and around the world. That being said, I do not want to suggest that the events of September 11 and all that has followed play only a small role in this book. It would be foolish, if not impossible, to approach this topic without including this most obvious and contemporary of examples. I do, however, want to stress that 9/11 will be viewed in the context of the larger issues presented by rhetoric and terrorism.

Second, you would be well served to search your own feelings about 9/11 and how "objective" you feel about the topic of terrorism and rhetoric. How did this event make you feel? Has it changed your view of the world or the United States' role in the world? Has it changed or altered the way you define terrorism? Has it affected your perception of who might be a terrorist? Where do these perceptions come from? Some of what you will read may challenge these perceptions or at least add to your knowledge of the subject generally.

Third, and feeding off this last point, this work is intended only to provide analytical tools and ideas for understanding what terrorism is and how its meaning is constructed. Nothing in this writing should ever be construed as an endorsement of violence and destruction, or a trivialization of the very real pain and suffering of its victims in any place or at any time. Of necessity, the study of this subject and its examples requires a sense of emotional distance—being able to look at the subject matter as an observer and not as someone affected by it. This is the conceit of much that is social science, and, on occasion, this emotional distance may be seen as implying a lack of compassion and empathy. That is not my intent in this work. Instead, by conceptualizing terrorism as communicative and rhetorical, I seek to broaden our perspective on this complex social issue by applying ideas from the field of communication studies.

I will argue later in this book that terror succeeds because it creates a sense of fear—a fear and dread of the unknown. Psychologists tell us that we fear and hate that which we do not understand. If such is the case, this book is offered primarily to engender understanding. If we understand how terrorism operates to affect us, we may approach a response to it that is not the product of our own fears but instead the result of reasoned and comprehensive thinking.

# 1

# The Struggle
# to Define Terrorism

In the past four decades, much has been written about terrorism and terrorists, some of it focused on the psychological profile of who the terrorist is,[1] what his or her motives are for engaging in terrorism,[2] and how governments should respond to it.[3] A lively debate has also ensued between academics, self-anointed experts, researchers, and many politicians as to what constitutes terrorism. This last point provides a useful starting place for our discussion in this chapter, as it provides a powerful intersection between rhetoric that defines terrorism and public discourse that is affected (and affects). To return to an earlier stated question: What exactly is terrorism?

## ❖ DEFINING TERRORISM

It should come as little or no surprise that the controversy over defining terrorism is long-standing in both the academic and the geopolitical senses. For decades, academicians and theorists have fared no better at defining the word than governments and the experts they employ. As I shall describe shortly, this has led to a multiplicity of possibilities and has created its own kind of chaos about the word. Chaos describes the state of things today, concerning definitions; but it does not help us in understanding how the word came to be so complicated.

## Tracing the Roots of the Word as a Label

Etymology is the study of the origin and evolution of words—in full recognition that language is organic, capable of change depending upon the needs of its users over time and place. Where did the word *terrorism* come from? The original use of the word in English is often believed to have derived from the Latin word *terrere*, meaning "to tremble." When combined with the French suffix *isme*, referencing "to practice," it becomes more like "to practice the trembling," or "to cause or create the trembling." *Trembling* here obviously is another word for fear, panic, and anxiety—what we today call terror. A group of revolutionaries called the Jacobins in France used the term when self-reflexively describing their own actions—and justifications—in the French Revolution. The meaning of this word in French was mentioned in 1798. The French, who for centuries have practiced a kind of cultural introspection, and have always been scrupulous about examining their language to purge it of useless words or to provide more precise definitions for words and expressions (and yes—they still follow this practice to this day!), in that year published the supplement for the dictionary of the Académie Française, in which the term was explained as the "système, regime de la terreur." The English version of this word as *terrorism* owes to an Englishman's characterization of the bloodshed he had observed from afar in France, where the same revolution was underway. Using an Anglicized version of the same word he had understood the Jacobins to use in describing their own behavior, Sir Edmund Burke wrote of the revolution in France and warned about "thousands of those hell hounds called terrorists" who were creating havoc and panic in the country.[4] Burke's book, entitled *Reflections on the Revolution in France,* reads less like a set of reflections and more like a set of criticisms. Beyond the usual cultural, nationalist motivations for his critique (he was, after all, an Englishman describing the French!)—at one moment, he describes the revolutionaries as a "college of armed fanatics" who mean to promote "assassination, robbery, fraud, faction, oppression, and impiety"—Burke's commentary must also be seen in the context of the social class position he occupied. As an aristocrat, Burke may have been concerned over the threat of the example made in France, where a popular, however violent, revolution had thrown out a monarchy and begun the elimination of the ruling class. Many countries with governments based upon monarchy, and with aristocratic classes supported by the crown, would in turn be threatened by this revolution to usher in popular rule and democracy. Though Burke did not himself define *terrorism* or *terrorist* in his *Reflections,* he as much as provided the definition by operationalizing it in several ways. In Burke's view, a terrorist was a *fanatic;* therefore, it could be inferred that a terrorist does not follow any means of logic or reason to justify his or her actions. Moreover, a terrorist was an *assassin*—a *murderer*—and a *thief,* and a *fraud*—not to mention an *oppressor.* None of these labels describes an individual whose characteristics could be admired or sympathized with. Murderers and thieves were and are criminals. Along with frauds and oppressors, they were and are viewed as lacking a moral center. In providing such an implicit comparison, Burke had begun the process of defining terrorism and terrorists and delegitimizing their behavior; but, as the reader may have noticed, the words *terrorism* and *terrorist* as Burke employed them were perhaps more labels than definitions.

As we shall see, more contemporary attempts at defining terrorism have focused on those against whom this violence is practiced. Much has been made in many definitions about terrorism targeting "innocents" or "noncombatants." In this capacity, it is also worth noting that the victims of the French Revolution (the period is often referred to as the Reign of Terror) were many, but chiefly those of the ruling aristocratic class. The vast majority were not military officers or officials of law enforcement. Indeed, those who lost their heads at the guillotine were often private citizens—what we might describe as civilians today. But to the revolutionaries, such distinctions would have been frivolous; for them, these individuals were not innocent or guiltless in any sense of the term. Although these victims had never raised an armed opposition to the revolution, they had benefited from the previous state of affairs in a system that brutally oppressed those of the lower classes.

Terrorism after that time came to reference a kind of violent, physical intimidation—real or merely threatened—designed to achieve some objective. In modern terms, we often think of such activity in criminal law as extortion: for example, a shop owner being forced to pay "protection money" to a local gang of young criminals in order to protect his business from destruction or molestation. Of course, in every extortion situation, the money is paid to protect the victim from the very individuals offering the protection!

Over time, however, the word *terrorist* was not used synonymously with *extortion*. Although terrorists might indeed be extortionists, it was not assumed that all extortionists were terrorists. The example initially provided by Burke supplied the difference in meaning, for critical in his use of the term that the Jacobins had themselves used was the *context* within which the label applied. The "hell hound" terrorists that he described followed a crude ideology, pursuing a political change by revolution. Thus, terrorism was tied to ideology and politics—usually, as in the French example, in a battle waged over power and control.

Throughout the next two centuries, *terrorism* was used often to describe violence in confrontations over power and control around the globe, including labor disputes and violent protest with management and ownership of the means of production; revolutions and armed struggles to overthrow or to achieve independence and statehood from foreign occupiers; and violent struggles over supremacy of ideologies, including those of anarchy, syndicalism, socialism, Marxism, communism, fascism, and capitalism. *Terrorism* was used to describe the activities of groups like the Molly Maguires (coal miners agitating for more rights), the Industrial Workers of the World, Bolsheviks, and many others. Ideological references for *terrorism* also extended to religion and began to include the battles waged between Islam and Judaism, as well as between Hinduism and Islam and between Christianity and all of the aforementioned groups. Common to all of these were the elements of violence *or the threat of violence,* often in a revolution or an armed struggle for control. Also critical to the use of the term was the notion that this use or threat of violence was in some manner outside the accepted norms or rules for war or battle. Of course, this last point in turn depended upon an additional factor in the evolution of the word—for it assumed that there were norms and standards for combat. Those who might follow such norms were usually thought to be those with organized, disciplined armed forces—soldiers who would play by the rules, according to some system of honor. Those with the means to wield such an armed force were, of course, nation-states, and as the aforementioned armed struggles suggest, it was nation-states who might ultimately become the targets of some kinds of terrorism.

Of course, it was and is possible that these same nation-states might themselves practice terrorism. Nearly every war offers examples of governments that terrorize civilians: the Assyrian empire, once the largest in the world, built by brutalizing all the peoples it conquered; Adolph Hitler's Third Reich, involving the systematic extermination of millions of Jews, Gypsies, gay people, Poles, and others; the actions of American Lieutenant William Calley in the massacre of an entire village of civilians at My Lai in Vietnam. History is filled with such examples, and over time, many who studied terrorism began to question why the use of this word referenced intimidation practiced by individuals against innocent victims, designed to coerce governments and nation-states, but did not seem to cover the multitude of examples of terror practiced by government upon other people.

From this question emerged a school of thought distinguishing terrorism *from below*, meaning terrorism practiced by those outside the dominant group, usually focusing their violence and threats on those above, and terrorism *from above*, referring to coercive intimidation practiced by the state directly or sponsored by the state indirectly and practiced by surrogates.

This kind of division allowed for a broader inclusion of types of terrorism, including individual or group dissent terrorism, criminal enterprise terrorism, and state-sponsored or direct state terrorism. Even with these distinctions, however, there was very little progress toward arriving at a precise and agreed-upon meaning for terrorism. Of course, language scholars might point out that many words are polysemic (capable of multiple or contradictory definitions),[5] but here the variety of possibilities only exacerbated the confusion over the meaning—largely because the meaning of the word depended rather heavily on *who* was providing the definition.

### Academic Definitions

Over time, academicians and theorists have suggested literally hundreds of different definitions for the word.[6] Though many of these definitions are similar, they are subtly different, often projecting an agenda for the author. For example, Martha Crenshaw has written that

> terrorism is a conspiratorial style of violence calculated to alter the attitudes and behavior of multitude audiences. It targets the few in a way that claims the attention of the many. Terrorism is not mass or collective violence but rather the direct activity of small groups.[7]

Though Crenshaw's definition recognizes that terrorism is directed to certain audiences, she also limits her definition to small group activity, effectively precluding any discussion of state-based terrorism.

Walter Laqueur, whose book *The Age of Terrorism* is considered by many to be a classic on the history of terrorism, has suggested that terrorism is the use or the threat of the use of violence, a method of combat, or a strategy to achieve certain targets. . . . [I]t aims to induce a state of fear in the victim, that is ruthless and does not conform with humanitarian rules. . . . [P]ublicity is an essential factor in the terrorist strategy.[8]

Laqueur's definition is both similar to and different from Crenshaw's. Note that both authors want to stay away from state-sponsored terrorism, although Laqueur acknowledges that states are capable of and have engaged in violence that might indeed be considered terrorist. He distinguishes them, however, by suggesting they do not employ terror on a systematic basis. Laqueur's definition here also raises the suggestion that there is some normative standard (which he calls "humanitarian rules") against which to judge what is normal and acceptable and what is unacceptable, abnormal—and terrorist.

By contrast, Annamarie Olivero, in her work *The State of Terror,* has argued that terrorism

contains its own rhetoric, which has been transformed throughout history by different states. By claiming to be defining a type of violence, i.e., one that threatened the site of legitimate violence (the state), it is clear that this term is reserved for the art of statecraft.[9]

From Olivero's perspective, the defining of terrorism is something in which states and their agents (including those in the academy) engage to distinguish illegitimate violence and dissent (practiced by those in opposition to the state) from legitimate violence and repression practiced by the state itself. In this way, terrorism is whatever violence is practiced against the state. Olivero, unlike Crenshaw and Laqueur, is quite clear that the defining of terrorism should and does include this kind of state-sponsored or practiced terror.

## State Definitions

The state itself has been no more consistent in defining terrorism than have members of the academy. For example, U.S. law defines terrorism as "premeditated, politically motivated violence against non-combatant targets by sub-national groups or clandestine agents."[10] Notice how the official legal version of this definition focuses on activity that is premeditated (intentional) political violence by *subnational groups or clandestine agents*; this definition focuses on violence that is done intentionally by groups at a substate level.

By contrast, the U.S. Department of Defense (DOD) has defined errorism as "the calculated use of violence or the threat of violence against individuals or property, to inculcate fear, intended to coerce or to intimidate government or societies in the pursuit of goals that are political, ideological or religious."[11] It might surprise you to see that different parts of the federal government define this term differently. Doubtless, this was one of the reasons encouraging President George W. Bush to urge reorganization of homeland defense in 2002, to coordinate flow of information between departments and agencies. How is this definition different from that at federal law? How is it the same?

Both definitions tend to limit terrorism to that *from below*—hardly a surprise. But notice how the DOD definition suggests that terrorism is designed to inculcate fear in the public—but with the purpose of intimidating or coercing the state. This definition suggests that terrorism creates political leverage from the frightened public to influence government or state policy. It also suggests that terrorism involves violence and destruction (against people or property) or the threat of the same.

But, as suggested, not all parts of the federal government are in agreement. As of the time of this writing (summer 2002), the Federal Bureau of Investigation (FBI) defines terrorism as "the unlawful use of force or violence against persons or property to intimidate or coerce a government, the civilian population, or any segment thereof, in further-ance of political or social objectives."[12] This definition starts out sound-ing similar to the others—but it concludes differently, for it extends the possible motives for a terrorist's behavior to include "social objectives."

## International Definitions

Globally, the community of nation-states is no closer to consensus on this definition than we are at home in the United States. For exam-ple, the United Nations has long struggled to define the concept. In 1937, the original League of Nations (the predecessor to the modern UN) drafted a definition of terrorism as "all criminal acts directed against a State and intended or calculated to create a state of terror in the minds of particular persons or a group of persons or the general public."[13] The convention never came into being, however—and to this day, the UN has no single, agreed-upon definition of the word, although there has continued to be considerable debate on the topic. An example of the kind of language the international community has considered can be seen in a draft resolution from a 1999 session of the UN. The resolution stated that the UN

1. *Strongly condemns* all acts, methods and practices of terrorism as criminal and unjustifiable, wherever and whomsoever committed;

2. *Reiterates* that criminal acts intended or calculated to provoke a state of terror in the general public, a group of persons or particular persons for political purposes are in any circumstance unjustifiable, whatever the considerations of a political, ideological, racial, ethnic, religious or other nature that may be invoked to justify them.[14]

As the large UN body continued to struggle for a definition of terrorism, it cobbled together 12 different piecemeal conventions and protocols. In 1992, a recommendation was made to the UN Crime Branch that terrorism simply be defined as the "peacetime equivalent of war crimes."[15] This also proved extremely controversial, however much more simple it might be to use. The UN body does not follow this definition today.

The European Union (henceforth EU), which initially seemed to take its cue from a desire to build an economic power to rival the United States, has found that with economic concerns come political questions. The EU, often the target for terrorist attacks in the past, and sometimes the hiding place for groups that practiced terrorism, has itself struggled with a definition for the word. Recently proposed language for a framework on fighting terrorism defined the term as

intentional acts, by their nature and context, which may be seriously damaging to a country or to an international organization, as defined under national law, where committed with the aim of (i) seriously intimidating a population, or (ii) unduly compelling a Government or international organization to perform or abstain from performing an act, or (iii) destabilizing or destroying the fundamental political, constitutional, economic or social structures of a country or international organization.[16]

Filling a desire among some EU member nations to be quite clear about what specific activity would qualify under this definition, however, proved more controversial. Additional language suggested that the above destruction or destabilization could be a result of "causing extensive damage to a Government or public facility, including an information system, a fixed platform located on a continental shelf [or] a public place or private property likely to put in danger human lives or produce considerable economic loss."[17] The inclusion of extra language such as the reference to "a fixed platform located on a continental shelf" was a direct reference to environmental groups' occupation protests on oil platforms in the North Sea—such as Greenpeace's occupation of the Brent Spa oil platform. Equally, the earlier references to "intentional acts" that seriously damaged the work of "an international organization" was seen by some to be an attempt to prevent trade unionists from demonstrating violently (as they had, for example, for 3 days in Genoa) at meetings of organizations such as the G-7, or now the G-8, or even the EU itself.

Critics were quick to point out that this degree of specificity in defining terrorism was nothing more than an overbroad attempt to censor political dissent and free expression of ideas. It proved just as vexing for the EU as the various attempts at defining had for the UN.

## How Terrorists Define Themselves

The perspectives of individuals labeled as terrorists do not provide much clarity on a definition either. Predictably, their perspectives are self-serving and just as controversial as any academic or nation-state/government's attempt at defining.

For example, the original Irish Republican Army (IRA) elected to call itself an "army" partly out of a desire to counter the label *terrorist*— or the idea that their protest was in some way illegitimate. The original document given to every new recruit for the IRA was called the *Green Book,* and it set forth clear expectations of what was to be given by new members, as well as an orientation regarding the violent activity of the organization. It began by stressing: "The Irish Republican Army, as the legal representatives of the Irish people, are morally justified in carrying out a campaign of resistance against foreign occupation forces and domestic collaborators."[18]

By calling themselves an "army" and "legal representatives," the IRA become more like a government or a nation-state representative. These word choices are rhetorical efforts aimed at conferring legitimacy and official status on their actions. The *Green Book* later speaks of the violence these new recruits must be expected to commit:

> Volunteers are expected to wage a military war of liberation against a numerically superior force. This involves the use of arms and explosives.
>
> Firstly, the use of arms. When volunteers are trained in the use of arms, they must fully understand that guns are dangerous, and

their main purpose is to take human life, in other words to kill people, and volunteers are trained to kill people.

It is not an easy thing to take up a gun and go out and kill some person without strong convictions or justification. The Army, its motivating force, is based upon strong convictions which bonds [sic] the Army into one force, and before any potential volunteer decides to join the Army he must have these strong convictions. Convictions which are strong enough to give him confidence to kill someone without hesitation and without regret. The same can be said about a bombing campaign.[19]

Nowhere in this telling passage is the word *terrorism* used. Instead, the violence—in the form of killing—is referenced as a "military war of liberation" against the British. Those who kill are not killers or terrorists. Instead, they are soldiers in an army, being told to follow orders and discipline in warfare, in ways that do not allow for individual conscience and second-guessing. Although these words may sound terrible when contrasted with the loss of life caused by IRA violence through the years, they are really no different from the words and ideas a professional armed force of a nation-state uses to indoctrinate its new members.

Another perspective of terrorism offered by the terrorist grows out of a willingness to dehumanize the victims of terror by treating them as objects. The following passage from a Ku Klux Klan member's speech to other Klan members makes reference to the bombing death of four African American children, comparing them to animals. The speaker says:

It wasn't no shame they was killed. Why? Because when I go out to kill rattle snakes, I don't make no difference between little rattle snakes and big rattle snakes because I know it is in the nature of all rattle snakes to be enemies and to poison me if they can. So, I kill 'em all, and if there's four less little niggers tonight, then I say, good for whoever planted the bomb. We're all better off.[20]

Again, note that the speaker, however shocking his words and sentiments may be for anyone outside the immediate audience, never uses the word *terrorism* but essentially justifies a terrorist act by comparing children to snakes, objects that can and have been killed by humans in self-defense.

In sum, these various perspectives, whether offered by academics, specialists, governments and their agencies, large or regional international organizations, or even terrorists themselves, provide only too many choices for defining terrorism and very little sense of consistency. What terrorism is depends upon who you are and why you are bothering to define it.

Such a reality has led some to suggest that even attempting to define the term can only provoke controversy and debate and will not be terribly useful in helping us understand how to respond to terrorism. Walter Laqueur, cited earlier in this chapter, has stated that no one definition of terrorism will ever suffice to fully explain and describe the activity.

❖  ATTEMPTS TO SYNTHESIZE A CONSENSUS DEFINITION

### Jenkins's Definition

In that spirit, some theorists have tried to capture a consensus of the definition by examining all definitions to see what parts they have in common. Brian Jenkins has worked for many years as a consultant on terrorism and counterterrorism security. He proposed what may be the simplest definition of terrorism, synthesizing what he believed were the most basic components of all definitions on the subject. Jenkins suggested that terrorism is the use or the threatened use of force designed to bring about a political change.[21] This definition, popular with many who look at terrorism and security issues, sidesteps the complexities of the many different definitions by simplifying and reducing the term to violence or threats of violence for political gain. Does this definition make more sense than the others?

Some prefer Jenkins's definition because they find comfort and comprehensiveness in its simplicity—for terrorism here is political violence—regardless of other motives, and irrespective of the nature of the target of the violence (civilian, law enforcement, or military personnel) or the perpetrator of the terror act (whether an individual, group, criminal enterprise, or state). Of course, under such a broad definition, many forms and examples of violence could be placed. There are no wars that do not involve political motivations and gain—and depending upon how the words *political* and *violence* themselves are defined and used, virtually any individual act of violence toward the state, or toward another individual, may be considered as terrorism. This kind of definition is thus overly broad—but surprisingly, it was almost precisely the way the British once defined the term when legislating against violence in England and Northern Ireland.[22]

What constitutes *political* in such a definition? Perhaps this references anything involving matters of state—for example, policies and laws of the government, or perhaps elections and candidates. Is something political because it is merely controversial? Or perhaps because it has the capacity to affect a great many people? Does being political refer to questions of oppression and domination, struggles for power, and resistance to authority?

Doubtless the reader will have already observed that there is an inherent looseness with the way this word is used today. Any of the ideas suggested above may form the basis for labeling something as "political." And most surely, the continued careless use of the term in expressions such as *political correctness* only serves to obscure the meaning even more.

Likewise, there is controversy over the meaning of *violence* as used in the definition of terrorism above. What constitutes violence in such a definition? Any act of physical aggression—or at the least, the threat of it? Possibly—but what do we then consider as physical aggression? Perhaps we may refer back to our criminal laws and definitions for assistance here. For example, in nearly all countries, there are standards for assault, battery, rape, attempted murder, and murder, any one of which may provide the basis for the physical aggression we call "violence." Though few would be likely to dispute that shooting or stabbing another individual would meet the standard necessary for violence in defining terrorism, what of the other forms of proscribed acts (or attempts) at aggression?

Should we consider rape an example of physical aggression necessary to define terrorism? Rape may be seen as a tool of oppression (men over women) and power (even men raping or being raped by other men) with an inherent politicality about it. At present, however, terrorism as defined by law does not include rape.

What of the other forms of aggression referenced above? Assault is usually defined as any kind of intentional offer of corporal injury against another individual.[23] This can range from grabbing someone at the elbow and pulling them to you, all the way to tackling someone, shoving them, pinning them against the wall, or hugging them. Battery, usually a companion for assault, involves an advanced form of aggression to physical violence—a punch or kick.[24]

So much so good; attacking and hitting someone might be seen as the kind of physical aggression necessary for terrorism. But if so, how should we consider an attack in the form of hitting someone in the face with a pie? In the past decade, numerous groups have resorted to pie throwing as a means of civil disobedience. In 1998, for example, a group of Belgian protestors attacked Microsoft founder Bill Gates with "a small armada of cream tarts . . . covering him in whipped cream."[25] Gates was reportedly "surprised and disappointed,"[26] although angry enough to wish them charged with assault and battery might be more accurate. For their part, the pie throwers (already notorious for doing this to other celebrities, officials, and politicians) asserted that their act of civil disobedience was also symbolic political speech—not to mention an attack on "self-important" people. If so, this kind of aggression (both assault and battery) as violence was most definitely also political—thus making it political violence. But would one consider it terrorism?

In truth, the feature of this definition that makes it so appealing—its simplicity—is also its most pronounced weakness. In reducing terrorism to political violence, one expands the field of possibilities for consideration. In such a world, there is little that would not be considered terrorism.

## Schmid's Definition

A second, slightly more complex approach to finding a synthesized, consensus definition may be found in the work of A. P. Schmid, whose advisory work for the UN was cited earlier. Schmid reached a conclusion similar to that of Laqueur, suggesting that because of the complexity and diversity of perspectives on terrorism, no one single definition may adequately describe what is occurring with this violence or threat of violence. Nevertheless, recognizing that there may be some commonalities in the different perspectives, Schmid conducted a review of the various definitions, finding some 22 components that they had in common to one degree or another. He then produced a synthesized definition, containing the most common of those 22 components. According to Schmid:

Terrorism is an anxiety-inspiring method of repeated violent action, employed by (semi-) clandestine individual, group or state actors, for idiosyncratic, criminal or political reasons, whereby—in contrast to assassination—the direct targets of violence are not the main targets. The immediate human victims of violence are generally chosen randomly (targets of opportunity) or selectively (representative or symbolic targets) from a target population, and serve as message generators. Threat- and violence-based communication processes between terrorist (organization), (imperiled) victims, and main targets are used to manipulate the main target (audience(s)), turning it into a target of terror, a target of demands, or a target of attention, depending on whether intimidation, coercion, or propaganda is primarily sought.[27]

In Schmid's calculus, terrorism is seen as more of a method or form of combat and struggle, attempted for a variety of reasons more complex than just the "political." Schmid's perspective also acknowledges that a variety of actors—including the state—can perform or at least sponsor terrorism. His definition also more neatly distinguishes between the immediate victims of terror (who may be selected randomly or on purpose) and the main audience for terrorism (the public and/or the state), in whom the immediate victims serve to leverage fear so as to bring about some kind of action or change desired by the terrorist.

Does this definition create any more clarity than the others? At one level, it is more inclusive than the others in that it recognizes that terrorism may be produced *from above* or *from below*. It thus provides some framework for lawmakers who want to find agreement between nations in defining and outlawing terrorism.

Additionally, Schmid's definition is comprehensive and complex, where Jenkins was simple and reductionist. In this definition of terrorism, Schmid very clearly states exactly what he means by terrorism, allowing for objectives including terror, demands, and attention, as well examining the means by which objectives are accomplished in intimidation, coercion, or propaganda.

Finally, Schmid's definition is, for our purposes in this book, a better fit because it also reinforces the notion that communication is involved with terrorism. Schmid as much as says so directly when he mentions "threat and violence-based communication processes" in his definition. In my judgment, this provides us with a good starting place for reconceptualizing terrorism. Laqueur, Jenkins, and many others are right[28]; it is almost impossible to find a single definition of terrorism that will satisfy everyone. Even Schmid's definition will be dismissed by those who reject the concept of state terrorism. But unlike those who find a definition of terrorism elusive and difficult, I believe that a different approach may be found if we dispense for the moment with questions of motive and agenda in the defining and instead use this last point about Schmid's definition as a starting place for our discussion.

## ❖ SUMMARY

In this chapter, we have examined how the definition of terrorism may vary widely between scholars and academics, as well as between nation-states and their agencies, international organizations, and even terrorists themselves. More broadly, we have seen how terrorism may be classified as being *from above* or *from below* and have placed it in the context of political violence. In the end, however, no clear consensus has developed in any of these communities about terrorism, although the definition offered by Schmid does provide us with an opportunity to reconsider terrorism in a new light, as a process of communication.

## ❖ NOTES

1. See, e.g., J. Margolin, "Psychological Perspectives in Terrorism," in *Terrorism: Interdisciplinary Perspectives*, ed. Yonah Alexander and Seymour Maxwell Finger (New York: John Jay Press, 1977).

2. See, e.g., Simon Reeve, *The New Jackals: Ramzi Yousef, Osama bin Laden and the Future of Terrorism* (Boston: Northeastern University Press, 1999).

3. See, e.g., Strobe Talbott and Nayan Chanda, *The Age of Terror: America and the World After September 11th* (New York: Basic Books, 2001).

4. Edmund Burke, *Reflections on the Revolution in France*, ed. C. C. O'Brien (1790; London: Penguin Books, 1969).

5. L. Ceccarelli, "Polysemy: Multiple Meanings in Rhetorical Criticism," *Quarterly Journal of Speech* 84 (1998): 395-415.

6. See, e.g., Omar Malik, *Enough of the Definition of Terrorism* (Washington, DC: Brookings Institute Press, 2001).

7. Martha Crenshaw, ed. *Terrorism in Context* (University Park: Penn State University Press, 1995); quoted excerpt retrieved December 16, 2002, from www.psupress.org/books/terrorismincontextexcerpts.html#what.

8. Walter Laqueur, *The Age of Terrorism*, 2d ed. (Boston: Little, Brown, 1987), p. 143.

9. Annamarie Olivero, *The State of Terror* (Albany: State University of New York Press, 1998), p. 142.

10.  22 U.S.C.A. § 2656 (d).

11.  See U.S. Department of Defense, DOD Directive 2000.12, Protection of DOD Resources Against Terrorist Acts, June 16, 1986, p. 15.

12.  The FBI definition flows directly from the Code of Federal Regulations: 28 C.F.R. § 085.

13.  See "Definitions of Terrorism," retrieved December 16, 2002, from UN Office on Drugs and Crime Web site: www.undcp.org/odccp/terrorism_definitions.html.

14.  General Assembly Resolution 51/210, Measures to Eliminate International Terrorism, 1999, quoted in "Definitions of Terrorism," retrieved December 28, 2002, from UN Office on Drugs and Crime Web site: www.undcp.org/odccp/terrorism_definitions.html.

15.  The recommendation was made by A. P. Schmid in a report to the Crime Branch as an attempt to simplify the definition and avoid the seemingly endless debate about the term.

16.  European Union, Article I of the Framework Agreement on Combating Terrorism, December 7, 2001, quoted in "EU Definition of 'Terrorism' Could Still Embrace Protests," retrieved December 18, 2002, from Statewatch Web site: www.statewatch.org/news/2001/dec/07terrdef.htm.

17.  Article I.e of the Framework Agreement on Combating Terrorism (Art. 3.f in the Commission Draft), quoted in ibid.

18.  Irish Republican Army, *The Green Book*, quoted in Tim Pat Coogan, *The IRA*, rev. ed. (New York: Palgrave Press, 2000), p. 545.

19.  Ibid., p. 547.

20.  See A. C. Rapoport, *Assassinations and Terrorism* (Toronto: T. H. Best, 1971), quoted in Maxwell Taylor, *The Terrorist* (London: Brassey's Defence, 1988), p. 99.

21.  Brian Jenkins, "The Who, What, Where, When and Why of Terrorism" (paper presented at the Detroit Police Department Conference on Urban Terrorism, Detroit, MI, November 1984).

22.  See, e.g., the British Prevention of Terrorism Act of 1974, which defined terrorism as "the use of violence for political ends, and includes any use of violence for the purpose of putting the public or any section of the public in fear."

23.  *State v. Stow*, 97 N.J.L. 349.

24.  *Goodrum v. State*, 60 Ga. 511.

25.  Sarah Lyall, "Philosopher of Pie, Craftily Creaming Pomposity," *New York Times*, April 20, 1998, retrieved May 1998 from www.nytimes.com.

26.  Ibid.

27.  Alex P. Schmid, *Political Terrorism: A Research Guide to Concepts, Theories, Data Bases and Literature* (New Brunswick, NJ: Transaction Press, 1983), p. 70.

28.  See, e.g., Jonathan R. White, *Terrorism*, 3d ed. (Belmont, CA: Wadsworth, 2002).

# 2

# Terrorism as a Communication Process With Rhetorical Dimensions

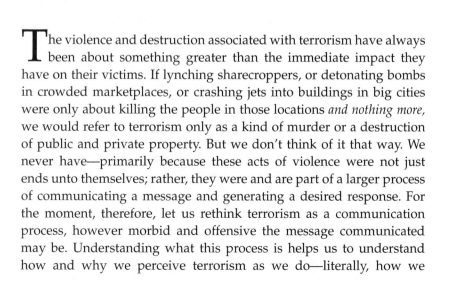

The violence and destruction associated with terrorism have always been about something greater than the immediate impact they have on their victims. If lynching sharecroppers, or detonating bombs in crowded marketplaces, or crashing jets into buildings in big cities were only about killing the people in those locations *and nothing more,* we would refer to terrorism only as a kind of murder or a destruction of public and private property. But we don't think of it that way. We never have—primarily because these acts of violence were not just ends unto themselves; rather, they were and are part of a larger process of communicating a message and generating a desired response. For the moment, therefore, let us rethink terrorism as a communication process, however morbid and offensive the message communicated may be. Understanding what this process is helps us to understand how and why we perceive terrorism as we do—literally, how we construct it and how it constructs our reality. What does this process look like?

## ❖ TERRORISM AS COMMUNICATION PROCESS

A simple model of communication suggests that human beings are senders and/or receivers of messages. In this most basic of approaches to human communication—relevant whether we consider how humans communicate in conversation, in public speaking, or even with semi-interactive, mass-mediated communication—a sender of a message *encodes* the message just before sending it, usually by reducing it to some kind of symbols (such as language—words, after all, are symbols), which is then sent to the person of the receiver, who in turn *decodes* it (translating and interpreting the symbols) and then considers it. If this process is described as *transactional* and *bidirectional*, the sender *sends* and *receives* messages, and the receiver does likewise.

If into this simple model of communication we place a terrorist as the sender of a message, and the public, an organization, a nation-state, or a government as the receiver, we find that the definition of terrorism can be more easily understood. This is in no way intended to trivialize the horror of death, pain, and suffering associated with terror violence; rather, here I am simply attempting to define terrorism differently for the sake of explaining how it works to affect us.

A terrorist sends a message to a target audience (the public, a nation-state, an organization, or the government) by engaging in an act of violence or destruction. The message is *not* the violence or destruction itself; rather, it is encoded within such activity. In this way, terrorism as a communication process has a rhetorical dimension that is independent of the simple coercion associated with violence for its own sake. Terrorism may or may not yield concessions. It may well serve to provoke discourse among target audiences. Or it may be a symbolic expression of the terrorist's rage or a demonstration of revenge. The process of encoding may depend upon the symbolic nature of the violence and destruction, as well as the potential for using different media to convey such a message.

The target audience decodes this message by relying upon the methods and tools it has for constructing its own sense of reality. These methods and tools may refer back to language and word choice, to discourse about the terrorism—often suggested by official government

**Figure 2.1**

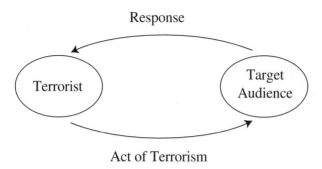

interpretations and responses of and to the message—and to discourse about how receivers of a mass-mediated message are to interpret and/or understand symbols of all kinds. We will explore each of these aspects in the following chapters. In practice, the process might look like what we see in Figure 2.1.

Though it is theoretically possible that a terrorist may operate within a communication process that he or she perceives as being unidirectional—such as one in which the terrorist communicates with violence and an ultimatum demand, threatening worse violence for noncompliance—the reality is that the terrorist message is still transactional and bidirectional because the first message generates some kind of response, which will always be communicated back to the terrorist either directly (in the form of government action, evidence of public discourse, etc.) or indirectly (via interpretation of the response through the media). Other audiences may be involved, adding to the size and complexity of the communication process. If such is the case, there are multiple audiences for the terrorist message, and these audiences may in turn communicate with one another and/or feed back independently or conjointly to the terrorist in the manner described above. This will, of course, alter the way we might envision this process diagrammatically (Figure 2.2).

Note that for the purposes of Figure 2.2, I have delineated four potential target audiences—but this is a random number only for illustration purposes here. There may be three or five or ten—the number is solely dependent upon the specific terrorist scenario.

Why would I suggest that multiple audiences may be involved with terrorism as a communication process? The answer to this

**Figure 2.2**

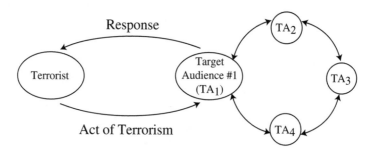

question takes us back to the definition of terrorism offered by Schmid. Recall that this definition recognized that terrorist violence and destruction may be inflicted against one target with the purpose of influencing another target audience. Schmid is absolutely correct in that assessment. When violence and destruction occur, the recipient of them is one kind of audience—though most likely not the primary audience. That primary audience will be those who witness and observe the violence and destruction and then engage in discourse about what they have seen. In many situations, that second, more primary target audience may be the public at large.

This occurs if the terrorist seeks a change in policy (e.g., forcing a targeted country to withdraw from occupation—as the Palestinians have long sought from Israel), demanding resources (e.g., ransom for hostages), or even seeking revenge (avenging the deaths of colleagues and comrades). In any of these situations, the primary public audience is targeted so that discourse and panic will ensue.

These individuals, in turn, will not constitute the only other audience. Indeed, government officials (if a state policy is implicated in the message) or institutional officials (if an organizational or institutional policy or practice is implicated in the message) will serve as a distinct but potentially overlapping target audience. The public audience will often be used (as suggested before) to leverage pressure against the government or institutional audience to change a policy or practice in complying with the terrorist demands. The public audience is distinct from the target audience upon whom the violence and destruction were inflicted, and both of these audiences will be distinct from the government or institutional audience, who may or may not respond with, for example, a change in policy.

Additionally, there may be other audiences in this process. These may include members and representatives of different kinds of media (broadcast, print, Internet, etc.), or potentially the public as constituted in other countries and cultures, or, for that matter, their governments or institutions. As to the latter, these other countries may be allies or enemies of the nation-state attacked in the terrorist violence. Just as the media (at least in democracies) attempt to act independently from the government of the state, so the government, institutions, and public of one country or culture will act independently from the government, institutions, and public of other countries or cultures.

To illustrate further, let us reconstitute the terrorism of September 11. Following this diagram, we might say al Qaeda terrorists launched their deadly attacks on New York and Washington, D.C., communicating a message with their violence and destruction on that fateful day. The first audiences were the recipients of that death and destruction— those who inhabited the Twin Towers (and the immediate surrounding areas in New York) in Manhattan, the employees at the Pentagon, and those unfortunate passengers on all flights involved during the day.

A second primary audience was the American public (like the students mentioned in the preface to this book), all of whom witnessed and were terrified by what they saw of the message played back for them repeatedly over television, on radio, and in print (especially in newspapers and magazines).

A third possible audience would be relevant officials in our federal and even state governments, who were required to respond to these attacks either by contemplating military or law enforcement responses, changes in foreign policy, changes in domestic security, or by generating messages of calm for the public. This audience could have included anyone from Mayor Rudolph Giuliani (and his staff) of New York City, to Governor Gray Davis (and other officials) in faraway California, all the way up to the White House and President Bush, Congress and relevant legislators, the Joint Chiefs of Staff and the military, and so forth.

An additional audience here would have been members of our own media, who operate (at least on the face of it) independently of what they are told by our government, as well as independently of the public to whom they offer news. Their response incorporated coverage and treatment of the terrorist message, as well as internal discourse about what to report and how to frame the multiple stories of that tragic day in September.

Other audiences included our allies (e.g., Great Britain), countries that might be neutral with respect to terrorism (e.g., some European countries), and groups that we might consider to be hostile (e.g., the Taliban in Afghanistan). Any and all of them were potential audiences for the violent, destructive message that day because any of them might be targets themselves or might be affected by whatever response the United States government eventually chose to make.

This is only a partial list of the potential audiences for that message on that day; can you think of other audiences for September 11?

As suggested before, these audiences in turn communicate with one another, individually and/or collectively, directly and indirectly, as part of the greater loop that can also feed back to the terrorist. In almost all situations, the connections between the different audiences were already established prior to the communication loop created by the terrorist message. When the various audiences communicate with one another, they will also engage in the encoding and decoding of messages, and any of them may communicate directly or indirectly (as part of the group of audiences) with the terrorist.

For example, this process could describe the ways survivors of the violence and destruction in New York communicated with people in the American public, often via broadcast and print media; or it could describe the ways President Bush or other representatives of his administration communicated with foreign heads of state and their publics, such as Tony Blair and the public at large in Great Britain; or it could describe the way the reaction of the American public was conveyed to other countries that might have sheltered, sponsored, and assisted in the terrorism of that day. Of course, any of these same messages could have been conveyed back to the terrorists within the same loop. In that way, Osama bin Laden or other members of al Qaeda would have seen and understood the American reaction—or at least a mediated summary of it—via satellite television from CNN or any number of media sources.

This description of the process is useful for discussing what happens with terrorism because it allows for any type of terrorism to be considered, regardless of ideological or political agendas behind the labels of terrorism. In that way, this conception of terrorism as a communication process could describe state-sponsored terror *from above* as easily as dissent terrorism *from below*. It would be equally relevant for describing William Calley's actions in allowing and participating in the massacre of civilians at My Lai (a direct or indirect—depending on whom you believe in the chain of command—form of state-sponsored terrorism) or the similar tactics of Russian troops in contemporary battle with Chechnyan fighters (also state-sponsored terror). It could easily describe the actions of groups like the Ku Klux Klan or the Aryan Brotherhood in attacking minorities or threatening violence against gays and lesbians, just as it could describe the efforts of drug cartels in South America or Asia that employ terror tactics to combat government efforts aimed at diminishing or eliminating the trafficking of drugs.

This much describes the outlines of terrorism as a process of communication, but it does not yet elaborate any details about how the communication occurs and how it is processed and responded to. For this portion of our inquiry, we must begin by going back to the purpose(s) for communicating with terrorism in the first place. At the beginning of the loop sequence, what are the objectives to be achieved from communicating?

Again, Schmid's definition provides some guidance here. At one level, the terrorist may be looking to create terror, panic, and chaos; or possibly to draw attention to an issue or condition that has been given scant or no treatment in media or world political forums; or perhaps to make the government or institution attacked or coerced by such action give in to the demands made by the terrorist. In any of these situations, however, we can see that the real goal of the communicated message in terrorism may be considered persuasion: to persuade audience members that chaos and fear will be their lot in life, to persuade them to pay attention to an issue they have ignored, or to persuade them to do something they might not otherwise do—such as persuading our government to rethink its support for Israel in the Middle East. Terrorism at this level also becomes about the business of persuading. Some would differ with this last point, seeing terrorism as coercion and suggesting that persuasion and coercion are different and distinct concepts.[1] But these distinctions ignore the fact that coercive terrorism is really just a different form of persuasion. If persuasion involves using rational arguments and logic to enable someone to reach a decision of his or her own free will, terrorism meets this standard as well. Those targeted can still use rational choice to decide whether they will give in, fight back, or simply suffer their punishment. When targets of terror make these decisions from the product of the discourse in the communication about terrorism, they are making rational choices, no differently than if they were listening to competing arguments before reaching a conclusion. In this way, at this level, terrorism is persuasion.

Consequently, to understand how the communication process operates and constructs terrorism for us (and by us), we must examine terrorism as persuasion—and assess its rhetorical dimensions.

## ❖ TERRORISM AND RHETORIC

As you have perhaps already observed, definitions of words can prove very controversial and contentious. This much was already seen in the myriad different and sometimes similar definitions of the word *terrorism*; it is also true of the word *rhetoric*. What does this word *rhetoric* mean—and, more important, how I am using it when suggesting that there are rhetorical dimensions to terrorism?

### Exploring the Meaning of *Rhetoric*

The term *rhetoric* as used in everyday language and discourse has a fairly simple meaning. When someone references a "politician's campaign rhetoric" or suggests that a statement was "only rhetoric, and not substantive," he or she is suggesting a meaning for rhetoric that associates it with words that have little purpose other than to persuade or manipulate. As a starting place, that is not necessarily accurate—although it does give us a place from which to build a working definition for our study of terrorism.

In my judgment, *rhetoric* refers to the manner in which symbols (including, but not limited to, words) are used to affect, influence, and persuade people. Any definition of rhetoric, however, will have its detractors and critics. Mine is no exception—and in the spirit of encouraging the reader to discover some meanings of this term, we will very briefly review the development of this word to modern times to see how I am using the word today.

Rhetoric was studied and practiced in ancient Greece, initially as a component of the practice of democracy by citizens of Athens, who were encouraged to gather and speak at public assemblies on issues facing the community. Public speaking in this realm involved more than delivery mechanics such as fluency, vocal volume, eye contact with the audience, or expressive gestures. Effective speaking at such assemblies also required mastery of issues, the ability to be articulate, and a sense of sophistication about mustering arguments to advocate one's position on these issues. Not coincidentally, today when we think of the word *sophisticated*, we think of something that is clever, elaborate, and detailed. But this word derives from the word *sophistry*, which described the practices of a group of Athenians known as Sophists, who believed and taught that public speaking was an art form and a virtue unto itself. Sophists became traveling teachers in this time, teaching others how to do public speaking and contrive arguments for persuasion. They were eventually criticized by many, including the philosopher Plato, who charged that Sophists believed in making arguments only for the sake of arguing and not because (to put it in terms we might understand today) there was anything of merit in the arguments themselves. Sophistry was thus ridiculed as empty rhetoric—making arguments that sounded clever and logical but were, in reality, specious. This initial assessment of sophistry created a belief that rhetoric itself was truly empty and perhaps only an attempt to appear clever for the sake of being argumentative.

Plato's view of rhetoric, however, was refined by his pupil Aristotle, who felt that the practice of rhetoric was something worthy of inquiry, investigation, and understanding, as much for those who would do rhetoric as for those who might be subjected to rhetoric. In a book written nearly 2,400 years ago,[2] Aristotle introduced readers to concepts of rhetoric—admittedly for public speaking purposes—that are still applicable today and are actually useful in assessing other forms of persuasive communication. Chief among these concepts were his suggestions that effective arguments typically contained one or more of three "species" of proofs: *ethos,* or credibility of the speaker; *logos,* or the appeal of logic and reason; and *pathos,* or the appeal of emotion.

In the first century B.C.E., in Rome, members of the governing Senate would often vehemently debate and argue about the issues of the day. A Roman politician and thinker named Cicero was a renowned and prolific writer about rhetoric. Like the Greeks, Cicero believed that rhetoric was best seen in the form of persuasive public speaking known as oratory.

This tradition of rhetoric and public speaking was not limited to Greece and Rome. From the time of K'ung-Fu-Tze (Confucius) in the fifth century B.C.E. until the end of the third century B.C.E., China experienced an intellectual climate that rivaled that of ancient Greece.[3] Scholars traveling among the states rhetorically advocated a variety of systems of political and economic philosophy.

Likewise, in 15th-century western Africa, traveling storytellers recited parables and humorous narratives, and in northeastern Africa,

Islamic scholars went on lecture tours and spoke to very large crowds at a single time.[4] On feast days in one African kingdom (near present-day Mali), it was traditional for a bard to dress in a bird's head mask and deliver a speech to persuade the king to live up to the high standards of his predecessors.[5] Indeed, rhetorical oratory skills were highly valued by Native Americans as well; oratorical ability was often deemed to be a better indication of leadership quality than just bravery in battle.[6]

The common thread in all of these references is the practice and spread of rhetoric as persuasion in a communication form mostly as public speaking, and nearly always with an application to self-governance and participation—or to governing, or perhaps to the significance of religious beliefs. This was a tradition that also played well in the New World—in colonial America. During the Great Awakening of the 1730s and 1740s, preachers sought to revive religious zeal, which had been waning in the colonies. George Whitefield, for example, traveled through the colonies and drew large crowds for his dynamic, oratorical sermons.[7] He preached in fields because churches were not large enough to accommodate the listeners.[8]

Passionate political oratory helped inspire the American revolution against the British. Patrick Henry, well known for his oratorical skills, concluded before the Virginia House of Burgesses in 1765 that if changes were not made, King George III could lose his head like other tyrants. Subsequently, colonists began gathering in churches, schools, town squares, and taverns to express their dissatisfaction with the British.[9] In December 1773, approximately 5,000 colonists crowded into Boston's Old South Church to hear Samuel Adams and others denounce the British tea tax.[10]

In this same period of time, also referred to as the Age of Reason, those who studied rhetoric began to rethink the original interpretations of what the word meant—and what it could be. Whereas some extended the original Greek and Roman ideas for rhetoric, others added to and expanded the possibilities for the term. For example, Richard Whately, writing about rhetoric and argumentation, suggested legal concepts of *presumption* and *burden of proof*. These concepts, which will be explored in greater detail in the next chapter, helped define the ground rules by which rhetoric could be used by competing *rhetors* (advocates using rhetoric in opposition to one another). This empowered the individuals practicing rhetoric as much as it widened the playing field for those who wished to use rhetoric. Whately wrote mostly assuming a legal context (the courts and the law) in Great

Britain for this form of rhetoric, but over time, his expansion of rhetoric would come to be used by anyone engaged in formal debate.[11]

In this same period, Giambattista Vico of Italy offered a new and more expansive construct of rhetoric. Vico's vision of rhetoric explored the relationship between human perceptions of reality and the signs we find in everyday life that affect that perception. Unique in Vico's contributions about rhetoric was that human reality was constructed and that this construction could be rhetorical. At a critical level, persuasion might still occur—just as it resulted from a public speech in any of the aforementioned examples—but here the persuasion might occur as we were persuaded by our sense of reality to feel one way or another about our life experiences.

British rhetorical theorist George Campbell built on this widening construct of rhetoric by further suggesting that rhetorical *signs* or *symbols* were not limited only to traditional texts of writing or public speaking. In point of fact, Campbell argued, human beings were capable of being affected and persuaded by everyday types of artifacts—not only traditional texts.

Into the 20th century, the concept of rhetoric continued to change and develop. Key to this change was the development of *rhetorical criticism*—the means by which observers of rhetoric might observe, analyze, and deconstruct traditional texts or other artifacts for their rhetorical possibilities. Among the many contributions here was that offered by rhetorical scholars who desired a return to *neoclassical theory* (a more contemporary version of Aristotle's original ideas about rhetoric, especially as to persuasion and oratory),[12] as well as that offered by those who advocated *dramatistic criticism*[13] (dramatism is concerned with what rhetoric reveals about human motivation, action, and linguistic reality; it derives from the analysis of drama); *feminist criticism*[14] (to quote Sonja Foss, "Rhetorical criticism done from a feminist perspective . . . is designed to analyze and evaluate the use of rhetoric to construct and maintain particular gender definitions for men and women")[15]; and *media-centered criticism* (this argues that the rhetorical symbols we use to construct our perception of reality should be analyzed in the context of the medium within which they occur—both entertainment and news media).[16]

## Connecting Terrorism and Rhetoric

Although the above brief history is *not* intended as a comprehensive treatment of rhetoric, it is intended to demonstrate that rhetoric, though still fundamentally communication as persuasion, is today seen as more than just the construction we find in public address as oratory. It can be found in any kind of text (both verbal and nonverbal) with symbols that give meaning to our reality. Central to understanding rhetoric for our purposes, therefore, is the identification of symbols in communication.

In the chapters that follow, we will examine rhetoric in terrorism by first returning to our discussion of *definition*, but this time focusing not on what terrorism is but on the purpose or motivation behind defining terrorism in the first place. Thereafter, we will examine the *act of terrorism*, treating the action as *symbolic* in its own right. How are the violence and destruction in terrorism symbolic—and ultimately discursive? Next, we will consider how the meaning of terrorism is negotiated through official *discourse*, with particular emphasis on the public address of government leaders. Finally, we will explore how our own preconceptions and discourse about terrorism are in turn primed by the symbols embedded within *media (both news and entertainment) depiction and interpretation of terrorism.*

In examining these areas where rhetoric and terrorism intersect, I will be drawing from some of the more relevant theories of rhetoric enumerated above. These include using theories of rhetorical presumption to help understand the defining of terrorism, theories that use acts of violence as texts to examine embedded symbolic meaning, a more modern version of neoclassical criticism to understand the public discourse about terror, and, later, media criticism to examine how the media prime public discourse regarding terrorism. Throughout our discussion of these, we will refer back to the various typologies of terrorism enumerated in the first chapter, including terrorism both *from above* and *from below*—dissent terrorism, state-sponsored terrorism, and criminal enterprise terrorism.

These components form what I have previously referenced as rhetorical strands, enveloping each connection in the communication process, as shown in Figure 2.3.

❖  SUMMARY

In this chapter, we have considered how terrorism may be constructed to have meaning beyond the immediate impact of its violence and/or destruction. To that end, we have examined how terrorism may be seen

**Figure 2.3**

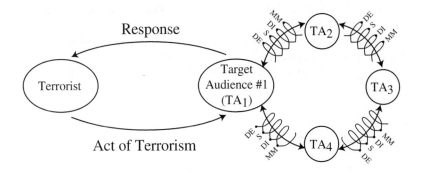

DE = Definition and Label
S = Symbols/Symbolism
DI = Discourse
MM = Mass Media

as a process of communication with messages for multiple target audiences. Seen in this light, terrorism involves persuasion directed to any of these target audiences—and this in turn suggests that there are rhetorical dimensions to the communication process involving terrorism. The concept of rhetoric has developed steadily over the past many centuries, and in this chapter, I have briefly reviewed some of this development, not to condense so much theory and history into a few pages, but rather to provide a context for using this term when applying it to terrorism and what I have labeled "rhetorical strands." In the coming chapters, we will examine how each of these strands contributes to the social construction of terrorism for any of its target audiences.

## ❖ NOTES

1. Some would prefer to define *coercion* as deterrence or compulsion but *persuasion* as the use of logic and reasoning to reach a decision with free will. See, e.g., Thomas Schelling, *Arms and Influence* (New Haven, CT: Yale University Press, 1966).

2. Aristotle, *On Rhetoric,* trans. George A. Kennedy (New York: Oxford University Press, 1991), p. 1356a.

3. D. Bodde, *China's First Unifier* (Hong Kong: Hong Kong University Press, 1967), p. 181.

4. A. A. Boahen, "Kingdoms of West Africa," in *From Freedom to Freedom,* ed. M. Bain and E. Lewis (New York: Random House, 1977).

5. G. Welch, "The Authors Who Talked," in Bain and Lewis, *From Freedom to Freedom,* p. 39.

6. C. Brooks, R. W. B. Lewis, and R. P. Warren, *American Literature: The Makers and the Making* (New York: St. Martin's Press, 1973), p. 1179.

7. A. Brinkley, *American History: A Survey,* 10th ed., vol. 1 (Burr Ridge, IL: McGraw-Hill, 1999).

8. N. Gabler, "Culture Wars: A Victim of the Third Great Awakening," *Los Angeles Times,* January 14, 2001, p. M1.

9. Brooks et al., *American Literature,* p. 1184.

10. P. Lewis, *The Grand Incendiary: A Biography of Samuel Adams* (New York: Dial Press, 1973), p. 180.

11. For a fuller description, see R. D. Rieke and M. O. Sillars, *Argumentation and Critical Decision Making,* 3d ed. (New York: Harper Collins, 1993), p. 23.

12. Much of this was based upon H. A. Wichelins, "The Literary Criticism of Oratory," in *Readings in Rhetorical Criticism,* ed. Carl Burghardt (State College, PA: Strata, 1995), p. 3. First published in 1925. For examples of essays employing this method of analysis, see W. N. Brigance, ed., *A History and Criticism of American Public Address,* vols. 1 and 2 (New York: Russell and Russell, 1943), and M. K. Hochmuth, ed., *A History and Criticism of American Public Address,* vol. 3 (New York: Russell and Russell, 1955).

13. See, e.g., Kenneth Burke, *The Philosophy of Literary Form: Studies in Symbolic Action,* 3d ed. (Berkeley: University of California Press, 1973).

14. See, e.g., Karlyn Kohrs Campbell, "The Rhetoric of Women's Liberation: An Oxymoron," *Quarterly Journal of Speech* 59 (1973): 74-86.

15. Sonja Foss, *Rhetorical Criticism: Exploration and Practice* (Prospect Heights, IL: Waveland Press, 1988), p. 151.

16. See, e.g., W. L. Bennett, *News: The Politics of Illusion,* 2d ed. (New York: Longman Press, 1988).

# 3

# Labeling and Defining
# Terrorism as Rhetoric

In the previous chapters, I have on occasion referenced the idea of our reality "being constructed," partially because the "meaning" of symbols has been "negotiated" through our discourse with one another. This concept of ongoing communication sees the process involved as transactional, and to the extent that meaning is negotiated, the process is also to some extent competitive. In some ways, it becomes a game.

Competitive games usually involve winning and losing and are governed by the rules of play. For example, a game may involve rules about boundaries, time limits, the number of players allowable, or players' conduct. By limiting and refining what players can do, these rules shape what the game will become. This notion of limiting, refining, and shaping a game applies equally well to the process of negotiating meaning in discourse through rhetoric. One very obvious application can be seen in the way definitions are created for discourse.

What is a *definition*? Why does it matter to discourse? In this chapter, we will attempt to answer this question, first by reviewing what a definition is and understanding how it is different from a *label*.

## ❖ DEFINITIONS AND LABELS

Definitions are (according to the definition of the word *definition*) nothing more than the precise, agreed-on, formal statements of the meaning of symbols. To define is to make the meaning of something clear. In Chapter 1, I presented numerous definitions of the word *terrorism*. Some (if not all) of these were summarized by Schmid's synthesized definition, which was to see terrorism as "an anxiety-inspiring method of repeated violent action, employed by (semi-) clandestine individual, group or state actors, for idiosyncratic, criminal or political reasons."[1] Defining terrorism in this way allegedly gives meaning to the word by beginning to shape the parameters of the term. According to this synthesized definition, terrorism inspires anxiety but does so with repeated acts of violence (as opposed to singular or random acts of violence). It is "employed," suggesting an intentional, strategic use, as opposed to a serendipitous, unintentional, or mistaken use. In this way, *terrorism* applies to those who target civilians or even military targets purposely but does not apply to accidental violence, such as the United States' accidental bombing of 30 Afghan civilians by a stray shelling of a wedding party.[2] Within Schmid's definition, however, *terrorism* might refer to the actions of a state (thus expanding the possibilities), but only when used systematically and intentionally. Definitions can expand possible meanings and/or contract them. This much describes definition. To define, however, is not necessarily to label. How are the two actions related—and why are they different?

In political communication, to label is to call something or someone by a name. *Terrorism* itself is, after all, a label. In this way, it is a name given to the meaning we associate from the definition above. Labels are distinct from definitions, however; although they give rise to definitions, they also play different roles in the process of discourse. In discourse, labeling provides quick, shorthand identification for whatever is labeled. Using the word *terrorism* to identify a violent attack on civilians in a marketplace gives this violence a quick and easily understood name. Definition, correspondingly, gives shape and narrows or broadens the application of that label and how it may be employed. The negotiation over what labels we should use and how we define their meaning produces different effects—especially when applied to political issues such as terrorism. First, negotiation creates possibilities for both empowering and marginalizing groups who are affected by labels and their definitions. Second, negotiation gives rise to flexible meanings, capable of both inclusiveness and exclusiveness for its users. Third, the end-product of negotiated meaning—the actual meaning or definition of the label—creates contrast between what is normal/acceptable and what is abnormal/unacceptable. As this negotiated meaning becomes operationalized by common practice and institutionalized by government laws and policy, a presumption of the correctness of the meaning settles in, effectively limiting further negotiation and debate.

In this chapter, I will discuss each of these effects, initially by considering parallel examples of similarly charged labels like *terrorism*; here I will examine the labels *hate* (as in *hate crime*) and *color* (as in *person of color*) to demonstrate the effects described above. Next, I will apply the same analysis to *terrorism* and will describe how the negotiated meaning of this label is part of a rhetorical process that has the ability to limit its debate and application.

## Definitions and Labels Can Empower
## and Marginalize: The Example of *Hate*

In political communication, definitions and labels create possibilities for empowering people, causes, issues, and movements—or taking power away from the same. One example of this can be found in the word *hate*. Dictionaries define *hate* as "an intense hostility and aversion usually deriving from fear, anger, or sense of injury,"[3] a descendant of the Old English word *hete*, akin to the Old High German word *haz*. Calling something an "intense hostility" or "aversion," however, is really no different from labeling it an emotion in the generic sense.

In modern parlance, we have come to see *hate* as much greater than a generic reference to hostility or aversion. Contextually, *hate* today refers to bigotry and prejudice, and specifically to bigotry in the presence of action—hence the use of terms such as *hate speech* and *hate crime*. In contemporary practice, this bigotry is directed at individuals on the basis of characteristics such as race, ethnicity, sexual preference, gender, and religion and now can also include disability status or even Vietnam-era veteran's status. Of course, this is much different from the original use of the word *hate* as described above. To refer back to our discussion about labels and definitions, this word became a label with a changing and expanding meaning. How and why did that happen?

Though etymology of the word *hate* traces it back to the Old English, as well as the Old High German, the modern usage of the term in the United States appears to have changed in the early 1970s. Research of various media sources shows that one of the earliest references to the term *hate* as bigotry or prejudice was probably made because of terminology introduced into public consciousness by the Anti-Defamation League (ADL).

This initial use of the label *hate* appears to have been more in reference to religious bigotry—and more specifically, anti-Semitism. Although he could credit no specific individual for the label *hate* as in *hate crime*, Ira Kaufman, then assistant director of the Central Pacific Region of the ADL, once told me that he believed the term had originated with the ADL, possibly in connection with anti-Semitic acts about which the ADL had been collecting data for many years.[4] Then-ADL board member and practicing attorney Brian Levin, a national expert on hate crimes, concurred in the hypothesis that originally this label was used in reference to anti-Semitism.

A lot of this came about because of the reporting (of these acts as crimes) . . . and to be honest, Jews in this country would be more likely to report these anti-Semitic crimes for two reasons. First, many of these hate crimes were property crimes, and you couldn't really do anything about it if you didn't report it. Second, Jews in this country didn't have the same distrust of law enforcement that other groups might have, so they wouldn't be reluctant to report.[5]

Levin's point was that American Jewish groups would be more likely to use the label *hate* in this way because they were one of the first groups to formally organize and track data about hate crimes.

By no coincidence, it was through the dogged persistent lobbying efforts of groups like the ADL that the U.S. Congress began addressing the issue of hate generally, and hate crimes specifically, culminating in the passage of such legislation as the Hate Crimes Statistics Act, enacted in 1990, which required the Department of Justice to acquire data on crimes that "manifest prejudice based upon race, religion, sexual orientation and ethnicity."[6]

The label *hate,* although not paired with the words *crime* or *speech,* could be found in references to anti-Semitism dating back to the early 1970s. For example, a 1973 article in the *New York Times* referred to "hate slogans" when discussing graffiti and vandalism on the walls of Temple Shalom in Brick Town, New Jersey.[7] References in this context were considerably less frequent in this period of time than they are now, although it was more common to see bigotry and prejudice labeled as "bias" or "community disorders"—the latter, a marvelously vacuous if not all together empty euphemism.

The New York City Police Department, for example, created a Bias Incident Investigation Unit (BIIU) in 1981, charged with investigation of bias-motivated crimes, from incidents like those occurring at Howard Beach and Bensonhurst. The city of Boston, by comparison, created a special unit in its police department called the "Community Disorders Unit," ostensibly for the same purposes. In the words of ex-New York Mayor Ed Koch, units such as these were created to ensure that crimes like "vandalism that consists of a swastika on a synagogue door . . . are treated differently than mere graffiti."[8]

Referring to bigotry and prejudice as "bias" continued to be common into the early part of the 1980s, but by the midpoint of that decade, it became more common to use the label *hate* to describe the same thing. For example, by 1985, even a comparatively conservative mainstream media publication such as *U.S. News and World Report* embraced this use of the label as it noted:

> At a time when Americans are recalling the deadly prejudices of World War II, a new wave of *hatred* [emphasis added] is building in their own back yard. Jews are targets, as they were in Germany four decades ago, but Blacks, Asians and Hispanics are also being hit.[9]

From roughly this point forward, as the above example illustrates, the label *hate* began to encompass other forms of bigotry and prejudice—including that directed at individuals on the basis of race and ethnicity. Today, we know that the list of those targeted by hate has grown and expanded—even to the point of including groups that might not otherwise be associated with one another.

It is possible to explain the public shift in the use of the label *hate* by looking back to the way an official or institutional embrace of the label *bias* at one time contributed to the official understanding of "bias motivation" as prejudice. It may be that federal laws like those that authorized data collection officially sanctioned and institutionalized the use of the *hate* label in public discourse. This much would be a part of the process of negotiating the use and meaning of labels. There is no doubting the potential of the law to act as a teacher for people in culture and society—but in this instance, such an explanation would be circular. What we label as hate today—bigotry and prejudice—did not begin in 1973, 1985, 1990, or 2002. Unfortunately, bigotry and prejudice are practices that precede these times by thousands of years of human history. So what else explains the use of this label to describe so many forms of bigotry?

One explanation might be that such labels can engage a sort of *umbrella effect* as more and more groups become empowered by and embrace the use of labels originally intended for a more limited group. As more people embrace the term as their own, the label increasingly gains public acceptance and currency in discourse, or, if the comparison is not too clumsy, as the umbrella spreads out, more people try to come under it for protection from the elements.

### Negotiating Definitions and Labels Creates Flexible Meaning: The Example of *Color*

On occasion, definitions for labels like *terrorism* may contract or expand, depending upon how their meaning is negotiated. When the meaning expands, the label becomes more inclusive and accessible to different users. When it contracts, the label becomes exclusive, effectively limiting those who may claim it. To illustrate this point, consider the label *color* as used in terms like *people of color.* The earliest possible references to the label *color* were almost exclusively reserved for race—and specifically for blacks of African descent. Indeed, the early use of *color,* as in calling a black American *colored* or *a colored person,* referenced the term this way in the pejorative. So common was the use of this label, however, that groups sensitive to the negative meaning in its definition nevertheless used the word in titles such as NAACP (National Association for the Advancement of Colored People).

In our society, labels like *colored person* and *Negro* were quickly replaced by *black* and later by *African American,* the latter of which still has currency today, although some groups have dropped any reference to *American,* preferring the label *person of African descent.* By the end of the 1980s and into the past decade, a new label had crept into public discourse when referencing members of this community: *people of color.*

Although the early context for this applied to African Americans, the sheer ambiguity in the label *color*—which in many ways meant something darker or different from white—meant that this label could be expanded to include nonblack groups that might otherwise be in positions of minority status relative to the dominant white majority. The list could then grow to include American Indians (Native or Indigenous Americans, as many now prefer to be called), Asian Americans, Hispanic or Latino Americans, Middle Eastern (as in Arab) Americans, Eskimo Americans, Pacific Islander and/or Samoan Americans, and so forth. In the end, *person of color* came to mean every kind of color—or, in reality, racial grouping (the term *color* is awfully imprecise)—except white European.

The expansiveness of the label pulled many groups into a kind of inclusive solidarity with one another that they might not otherwise—owing to cultural and political differences—enjoy. The label has empowered these groups by drawing them to one another, as individual minority groups have become a larger collective minority group. In many respects, that is its attractiveness.

What the examples of both *hate* and *people of color* demonstrate is that the labels we employ may change over time as their definable meaning becomes negotiated by discourse and normal use. Part of that negotiation involves the inclusiveness or exclusiveness of the intended meaning. Can the definition behind a label be expanded, or is it inherently limited? In the cases of *hate* and *people of color*, the definitions were capable of expansion. With *terrorism*, the meaning is still being negotiated—although at this point, it is safe to say that most legal definitions (especially in this country) are not inclusive of terrorism *from above* and thus limit the meaning of the label.

## Definitions, Labels, and the "Opposite of Normal"

An additional feature of labels and the definitions that supply their meaning in the political context is that they provide us with a point of reference for comparison. Often, labels like *terrorism* give meaning to what is abnormal and unacceptable by providing an implicit comparison to what is normal and acceptable, thus reinforcing a preference for the latter over the former. How does this work? Before looking to terrorism, let me return for the moment to the label of *hate*.

An additional appeal of this label (instead of *bigotry* or *prejudice*) owes more to the psychological understanding of hate and its manifestation in human behavior. Unlike political scientists or rhetoricians, psychologists often define hate simply in the context of emotion. For example, hate has been defined as a "hostile emotion, combining feelings of detestation, anger, and a desire to retaliate for real or fancied harm."[10] As an emotion, it has also been defined as "a state of arousal or excitation in humans, in which anger, negative judgments, and impulses of destruction predominate."[11]

Though hate is not itself viewed as innate to the human constitution, it is nevertheless thought to be "indirectly innate"[12] through its association with the emotion of anger and the impulse to aggression, both of which have been described as innate human characteristics. These have been observed in the ancient practice of hunting and gathering for primitive humans, territorial separation of groups and individuals, strife and conflict between the same, and the creation of hierarchies by social order, class, and division.

Biologists might explain this by associating hate and aggression with the "fight or flight" syndrome, a response arousing the sympathetic nervous system and the endocrine system. With fight or flight, the person manifesting those biological reactions now has an emotional reaction, with the option of engaging the source of the stress or fleeing from it. In the words of Gerald Schoenewolf, "Hate is the cognitive component of the fight or flight arousal state. The state of aggressive arousal differs from other states of excitement such as anxiety or nervous anticipation. . . . We hate that which frightens, frustrates or unsettles us."[13]

If, as Schoenewolf suggests, we hate that which frightens, frustrates, or unsettles us, and hate is a hostile emotion combining anger and aggression, hostility and detestation, then we can perhaps explain the use of this as a label when seeing hate in the context of bigotry and prejudice. Although it is surely an overstatement of the psychological definition to say that all prejudice and bigotry is hate, we may safely assert that within the confines of bigotry or prejudice rest the potential for anger, negative judgment, and the impulse to aggression or destructive action. The popularization of the term *hate* for bigotry and prejudice may then be explained as an extension of the public willingness to control emotion, to subjugate that which is nonrational to that which is reasoned and rational.

In our society, we teach our children from the time they are young that temper tantrums and uncontrolled outbursts of rage are improper behavior. We reinforce our parental teaching with social rules—in our schools—about civility and orderly conduct. In the curriculum that we offer students, and later in the rules that we follow in life, we emphasize reasoned discourse in decision making. We are critical of emotional responses, even if, by emphasizing what is rational, we go against our own biological tendencies. When adults act in anger or frustration, we may empathize, but we are critical of their failure to control these emotions. If their action is successful, we do not praise the emotion that motivated it; rather, we characterize it as risky and label them "lucky" in the circumstances.

Thus, it is possible that we have labeled this form of bigotry and prejudice as hate because we think of hate as emotion, and emotion is something we can and want to control. It is, after all, far easier to rationalize laws that regulate hate-motivated conduct or expression if we conceptualize hate as emotion and not as an individual belief or idea. The end result of this defined meaning for the label *hate* is that it also succeeds by providing an implicit comparison between that which is normal, desirable, and acceptable (reasoned discourse, control, rational decision making) and that which is abnormal, unacceptable, and undesirable (hate as emotion, giving rise to anger, aggression, detestation, and possible destructive action). Labels and the definitions that give them meaning provide those contrasts. The same applies as we now look back at the definition and label of terrorism.

## ❖ RECONSIDERING THE DEFINITION OF TERRORISM

Placing Schmid's synthesized definition of terrorism in the context of the above discussion, we can see that the actual definition is not as important as the purposes for defining terrorism in the first place. Definitions have several effects: They empower and marginalize at the same time; they create a contrast between us and what I will term "the other"; and, finally, they become legitimized rhetorically by the theory of presumption.

### Definitions, Labels, and Empowerment/Marginalization

As indicated above, one effect of providing a definition for a label involves the role of power—how it is rhetorically given and how it can be taken away. The labels *hate* and *color* both had meanings with the inherent capacity to empower audiences. When the word *hate* grew to include many minority groups (on the basis of race, ethnicity, religion, sexuality, disability status, etc.), every one of these groups became stronger by becoming part of a larger, collective whole. Politically, this larger body became empowered—to the point where today Congress and all state legislatures have been forced to seriously reconsider hate crime, and to a lesser degree hate speech, and the role that laws might play in eradicating the problem they cause. Likewise, expanding the definition of *color* in *people of color* to mean "groups of other than white European descent" dramatically increased the number and political power of people within that category, again forging alliances (or the perception of them, anyway) between groups that might not otherwise have had reason or opportunity to combine forces.

In the definition of terrorism, there is also an effect upon power—although this time, the redistributive effect of power occurs between the groups of the victims and the terrorists/aggressors. In many situations (if we are referencing dissent terrorism), the terrorists/aggressors begin in the role of those who are already oppressed or who have the self-perception of being in such condition. When engaging in terror as a means of fighting back against a perceived oppression, the terrorists reverse the power relationship in that moment, for they now control life and death, destruction or tranquility. The victims, formerly perceived by the terrorists to be in a position benefiting from oppression or the like, are now in the position of becoming the oppressed. Being able to define the act of aggression (violence and/or destruction), however, empowers the victims of terrorism. Why? Because being able to define the violence and/or destruction allows the victim to label it—and the label itself delegitimizes the action.

In the same breath, the act of defining and labeling the action as terrorism also marginalizes the terrorists/aggressors, for it precludes any possibility of legitimacy for their cause or sympathy for their actions. Terrorists are seen as playing outside the rules, without honor, attacking the innocent and weak, who cannot defend themselves. At least, that is the inference drawn from the characterization once the process of defining and labeling has begun.

### Terrorism and the Other

Kenneth Burke suggested that language conveys action and content, reflecting a rhetor's attitudes, values, and worldviews.[14] Burke also recognized, quite accurately, that all political movements and conflicts inevitably require lines to be drawn, sides to be defined, and allegiances (or their absence) declared. In analyzing Adolph Hitler's *Mein Kampf*, he noted:

> If a movement must have its Rome, it must also have its devil. For as Russell pointed out years ago, an important ingredient of unity in the Middle Ages (an ingredient that long did its unifying work despite the many factors driving towards disunity) was the symbol of a *common enemy*, the Prince of Evil himself. Men who can unite on nothing else can unite on the basis of a foe shared by all.[15]

Burke then cited directly from the writing of a younger Hitler, who had written in *Mein Kampf*:

As a whole, and at all times, the efficiency of the truly national leader consists primarily in preventing the division of the people, and always in concentrating it on a single enemy. The more uniformly the fighting will of a people is put into action, the greater will be the magnetic force of the movement and the more powerful the impetus of the blow. It is part of the genius of a great leader to make adversaries of different field appear as belonging to one category only, because to weak and unstable characters the knowledge that there are various enemies will lead only too easily to incipient doubts as to their own cause.

As soon as the wavering masses find themselves confronted with too many enemies, objectivity steps in, and the question is raised whether actually all the others are wrong and their own nation or their own movement alone is right.

Also with this comes the first paralysis of their own strength. Therefore, a number of essentially different enemies must always be regarded as one in such a way that in the opinion of the mass of one's own adherents the war is being waged against one enemy alone. This strengthens the belief in one's own cause and increases one's bitterness against the attacker.[16]

Tragically, history teaches us that Hitler's *one enemy* was the "international Jew," as scapegoating and eventually murdering millions of Jews became the powerful, horrific "blow" he alluded to in this earlier phase of his life. Burke's larger point in studying Hitler's words is that this single focus on a common foe—what Burke refers to as a rhetorical "unification device"—is a powerful tool for galvanizing the masses and keeping one's own people from questioning or second-guessing a leader. Burke concludes his analysis with a warning for all people to more critically evaluate the rhetoric our leaders use in constructing such enemies.

An important feature of definitions and the labels to which they supply meaning, as suggested earlier, is to create an implicit contrast and comparison between what is normal, acceptable, and desirable and what is abnormal, unacceptable, and undesirable. This allows the audience for such rhetoric to distinguish between the in-group and the outsider—the other.

The act of defining terrorism, if considered in this light, provides an opportunity for a contrast between us and our enemies, or enemy: the outsider, the other. In many respects, the drawing of this contrast is more important than the definition of terrorism itself. Further, the definition is not the only place this contrast is made; rather, it is a starting place. To give the contrast more impact, we must also negotiate the meaning of terrorism through our own discourse, which includes the other rhetorical strands that we will explore in the coming chapters. For now, it is enough to point out that a first purpose of defining terrorism is to suggest a distinction between us and the other—the terrorist.

### Definition of Terrorism and the Theory of Presumption

A third purpose served by defining and labeling terrorism has to do with the theory of presumption. As stated earlier in this book, presumption is shorthand for a theory of rhetoric developed by Richard Whately, asserting that the status quo (the way things are) would be preserved and presumed correct if an initiator of a claim for change could not meet his or her burden of proof in showing that change must occur.

Whately's original argument, used to place stress on the need for evidencing claims made in argument, was initially used in places where people practiced rhetoric in his day—in the legal system. As a legal theory, it can still be found in use today. For example, in a case involving *criminal law,* the accused will be presumed innocent until proven guilty. In a civil law dispute, the plaintiff bears the burden of proof in a claim of liability against the defendant; without such, we presume the innocence of the defendant.

Over time, people have continued using this theory (about presumption) in argument and discourse about government and politics, as well as other aspects of law. In the teaching of traditional forms of debate for students, the concept of presumption is still very much in play, whether students debate propositions of policy or propositions of value.[17]

By defining an act as terrorism, we as much limit the debate and negotiation we can have about this subject in discourse because the range of possible acts and motives that constitute this definition has been limited as well. Our tradition in Western culture of using the concept of presumption then rhetorically supports and reinforces the correctness of this definition in practice, effectively limiting discourse and making it very difficult for those who would challenge or seek to expand the definition. In the course of affairs, we become aware of the inconsistencies and contradictions about terrorism. What Basque separatists do to the Spanish government is terrorism, but a French government-sponsored attack on a boat belonging to Greenpeace environmentalists is only a tragic mistake. What the Chechens do to Russians is terrorism, but what Russian troops do in the war with Chechnya is the tragic consequence of a legitimate war. What Palestinians do to Israel is terrorism, but what the Israeli army does in shooting a rock-throwing Palestinian child or an innocent woman answering the door to an apartment suspected (incorrectly) of housing Hamas sympathizers is an unfortunate mistake.

The act of discourse allows us to recognize these as contradictions, but the notion of presumption prevents the discourse from doing more than recognizing. This occurs because the legal definition of terrorism is institutionalized by law and government practice—and presumption recognizes and supports it as the status quo.

## ❖ SUMMARY

Defining a concept such as terrorism is an important first step in seeing how terrorism is fundamentally a communicative process with rhetorical possibilities. Defining is related to but different from labeling. When we label something—like an action of some kind—we give a name to it. When we define it, we supply meaning for that label. Defining can be crucial in political communication because the definition of an act or concept can expand or contract (depending upon its final form), and such an end result can dramatically limit and shape the amount and nature of discourse about the same. For various reasons, definitions may be very expansive or extremely narrow. Definitions also provide contrast between what is normal and acceptable and what is abnormal and unacceptable.

The current definitions of terrorism—even that offered by Schmid—are similarly rhetorical. Schmid's definition, for example, provides an implicit contrast between what is normal or acceptable action and what is abnormal and unacceptable. The definition also allows a victim of terror to become empowered by the act of defining—and while it does this, it similarly acts to marginalize or rhetorically take power back from the terrorist. Presumption, as a rhetorical theory, then supports and reinforces the correctness of such a definition, effectively limiting further discourse about terrorism.

As suggested earlier, the reasons and purposes served by defining terrorism have tremendous significance for beginning to understand how this concept is communicative and rhetorical. In the next chapter, we will explore how an action that is violent and/or destructive—fitting within the definitions for terrorism—can itself be communicative and rhetorical.

### ❖ NOTES

1. Alex P. Schmid, *Political Terrorism: A Research Guide to Concepts, Theories, Data Bases and Literature* (New Brunswick, NJ: Transaction Press, 1983), p. 70.

2. "Villagers Recount Terror of US Air Raid," *New York Times*, July 4, 2002, p. A6.

3. See, e.g., *Merriam-Webster's Collegiate Dictionary*, 10th ed. (Springfield, MA: Merriam-Webster, 1993), p. 532.

4. In a telephone interview with Ira Kaufman in September 1994, Mr. Kaufman reported having spoken with more senior members of ADL, including Mike Lieberman, who noted that the ADL had started using the term in its publications at least "back into the mid-eighties," by which point the context for hate and anti-Semitism was already established and accepted.

5. Interview with Brian Levin, September 1994.

6. Federal Bureau of Investigation, *Summary Reporting System, National Incident Based Reporting System: Hate Crime Data Collection Guidelines* (Washington, DC: U.S. Department of Justice, 1991), p. 1.

7. *New York Times*, May 22, 1973, p. 45.

8. Edward Koch, "Toward One Nation, Indivisible," *New York Times*, June 26, 1987, p. A27.

9. Ted Gest, "Sudden Rise of Hate Groups Spurs Federal Crackdown," *U.S. News & World Report*, May 6, 1985, p. 68.

10. Robert Goldenson, ed., *Longman Dictionary of Psychology and Psychiatry* (New York: Longman Press, 1984), p. 335.

11. Gerald Schoenewolf, "Hate," in *The Encyclopedia of Human Behavior*, vol. 2 (New York: Academic Press, 1994), p. 501.

12. Ibid.

13. Ibid., p. 502. See also Sigmund Freud, *Civilization and Its Discontents* (London: Hogarth Press, 1930); I. Eibl-Eibesfeldt, *Love and Hate: The Natural History of Behavior Patterns* (New York: Shocken, 1974); Gerald Schoenewolf, *The Art of Hating* (Northvale, NJ: Jason Aronson Press, 1991).

14. Kenneth Burke, *A Grammar of Motives* (1945; Berkeley: University of California Press, 1969), p. xxii.

15.  Kenneth Burke, "The Rhetoric of Hitler's 'Battle,'" in *The Philosophy of Literary Form: Studies in Symbolic Action*, 3rd ed., rev. (Berkeley: University of California Press, 1973), p. 122.

16.  Adolph Hitler, *Mein Kampf*, quoted in Burke, "Rhetoric of Hitler's 'Battle,'" p. 122.

17.  Joseph Tuman, "Natural Value Hierarchies and Presumption: Merging Stipulated Artificial Presumption With Natural/Psychological Presumption," in *CEDA Yearbook*, vol. 13, ed. Ann Gill (Dubuque, IA: Kendall Hunt, 1992), p. 10.

# 4

# Symbols, Symbolism, and Terrorism

The U.S. Supreme Court long ago correctly recognized that almost any form of nonverbal behavior or action can be potentially expressive,[1] even if not always protected in the United States as a form of free expression. Although the Court's focus here was on distinguishing protected expression from unprotected expression, its point was relevant for our discussion about terrorism because conduct and action can be expressive—most commonly as symbolism.

In this chapter, we will examine how the actual acts of terror violence and destruction are themselves communication with a rhetorical dimension. We will also explore how symbols can be found in the tools and implements of terror, as well as in the targets of terrorism. The word *symbol* derives from the Latin *symbolum*, referring to a token of identity. In modern use, when we describe something as a symbol or declare that it possesses symbolic value, we are suggesting that this thing—whether an object, a word, a sound, or conduct—may be interpreted to mean something more than itself. How is it, then, that terrorism as violence and destruction means more than—violence and destruction?

## ❖ SYMBOLS, SYMBOLISM, AND VIOLENCE/DESTRUCTION

Though a seemingly limitless range of objects, actions, words, and signs may be construed as symbolic, three criteria help us to know when a symbol is in play. The first of these is *intent of the communicator/rhetor.* Here we would ask: Does the individual who employs a symbol intend for it to be interpreted in a particular way? Where there is evidence of such intent, the case for treating the act or object (or threat of the same) as symbolic and expressive will be stronger. Does the absence of intent suggest that there is no symbolic meaning? Suppose an individual employs a symbol without intending to do so? For example, in a nonterrorism setting, suppose that you merely wish to engage in the nonverbal behavior of walking on a sidewalk from one end of a block to the other. In this scenario, further suppose that the sidewalk cuts across an area that is police restricted for security purposes but that you are unaware of this. If you cross this line in ignorance of the restriction, can your walk still be construed as a form of symbolic protest and civil disobedience against the police? Or must you know that your act is unlawful and intend that observers will consider it as protest for your conduct to be considered symbolic? Some speech communication theorists distinguish message behavior from nonmessage behavior on the basis of intent,[2] whereas others believe that all behavior is communication if it is interpreted by someone in a meaningful way.[3] The latter of these perspectives makes better sense when we apply the question of intent to determining symbols in actions such as terrorism. Clearly, expressed intent of the communicator/rhetor terrorist—such as a call to "take credit" for a bombing, in which the caller explains the reasoning and meaning of the attack—will be clear evidence that the explosion is intended as symbolic. But the lack of such intent does not mean that an act or object is not symbolic. As will be seen, an action or object may become symbolic for the audience depending upon how the meaning of such a symbol is interpreted and negotiated by those who receive it.

A second criterion we may employ in considering a symbol is *context of the communication.* Here we would ask: What is the context for this symbol? Regardless of intent, objects and action may have different consequences for symbolic value when considered in different contexts. For our purposes, *context* refers to the situation within which the symbol occurs. This can include the surrounding environment, the timing, the audience and its background, and so forth. To extend the earlier example, if you are accompanied on the sidewalk by many other pedestrians, the symbolic value of the action may be very different than if you walk the street with others who are carrying signs and placards protesting the cruel treatment of animals at a business housed in the building on the street. And if you walk with these people, though never carrying a sign yourself, your actions may still have symbolic significance just by your presence at that particular moment. Context, therefore, is a significant consideration for determining the symbolic worth of nonverbal communication. When we apply this to terrorism, we look to the context within which the terror violence and destruction—or even just the threat of it—occurs. Where does the act or threat of terror occur? Who is the target audience? Within this environment, what are the means by which the terrorism takes place? What is the timing for the attack or threat, and how may that affect the way the intended audience perceives the terror?

A third criterion for examining symbolic value is *relativity of the symbolic message*. Here we ask: What are the relative effects of the message on different audience members? It may be argued that regardless of intent and context, symbolic meaning is at best an amorphous concept because of its relative effects. Different people may see and interpret the same action in entirely different ways. The way we, as receivers, interpret messages we receive is a relative consideration. Each of us may indeed look at the same act or object and see it entirely differently. Of relevance here for terrorism is whether those in one of the audiences for the terror (and there will often be more than one audience) will perceive and interpret the symbolic meaning in the same way.

At one level, terrorism may be seen as violent action and destructive consequences on a small or large scale, with loss of life, personal injury, or destruction of property. Some may wonder: Where is the symbolic message in such activity? Indeed, why isn't a punch just a punch? A kick, just a kick? A shooting or an explosion—just a shooting or explosion? Freud once suggested that thoughts and fantasies were symbolic representations of actions, such that they could precede actions and substitute for them as well. Dr. James Gilligan, a director of the Center for the Study of Violence at Harvard Medical School, has argued in response to Freud that

> the opposite is also true. Actions are symbolic representations of thoughts. That is, actions can precede and serve as substitutes for conscious thoughts. They can take the place of thinking in words,

if the behavior is never interpreted or translated into words and ideas. . . . Burke wrote that . . . we must learn to interpret language as symbolic action. I am suggesting that in order to understand violence we must reverse that procedure and learn to interpret *action as symbolic language*—with a symbolic logic of its own.[4]

What is the symbolic language of terrorism?

### Timothy McVeigh and the Oklahoma City Bombing

Possibly, we might explore the acts of violence as demonstrations of the feelings and emotions of those who commit them. With dissent terrorism (terrorism *from below*), the act of violence and destruction may be seen as the symbolic expression of rage. For example, the explosion that destroyed a federal building and killed 168 innocent people, including children, at Oklahoma City was eventually linked to an American named Timothy McVeigh. With the help of Terry Nichols, McVeigh's accomplice turned state witness, McVeigh was convicted in 1997 and executed for the heinous deed in 2001. His was an act, incidentally, that was first blamed on terrorist groups from other countries and then attributed to someone from the United States in what was labeled "domestic terrorism."

At trial, McVeigh's attorneys did not attempt to contest the physical evidence (McVeigh and the truck, the explosive material, etc.) or the mostly circumstantial evidence (there were no eyewitnesses who could place McVeigh at the scene of the crime but plenty who could describe McVeigh's motives and role in the affair) but instead chose to try and paint a sympathetic portrait of the man with testimony from family and friends in an attempt to humanize him. They then explained his actions as symbolic of the rage he felt against the federal government in general—and the Bureau of Alcohol, Tobacco and Firearms (BATF) specifically—for its role in the deaths of some 70 American members of the Branch Davidian compound at Waco, Texas, during a long assault by FBI and BATF agents. In his own mind, McVeigh's act was symbolic of his rage over the suffering inflicted by his own government. At trial, prosecutors made much of the T-shirt McVeigh had worn on the day he drove the truck to the Murrah Federal Building in Oklahoma City. On the shirt were written Thomas Paine's famous words: "The tree of liberty must be refreshed from time to time with the blood of patriots and tyrants."

## The Japanese Red Army

Another possible way to interpret the language of terrorism as an act of violence and/or destruction is to consider its threat potential—the terror act as a symbol of future threat. When terrorists strike in a public place, or in a fashion with potential for publicity, the message for those who witness the terror is often that this can happen to you too—next time. Whereas some targets are chosen purposely for this effect, at times, the random selection of targets makes this message all the more terrifying, creating the impression that terrorism can strike anywhere, any time.

This can occur when the terrorist strikes the public or even when terrorists turn on their own. For example, the Japanese Red Army, a terror group that emerged from the period of student unrest at universities around the world in the 1960s, was initially created to follow in the example of a West German terrorist group with the same name (Red Army)—hence the reason that the Japanese version required the word *Japanese* in the title. The Japanese Red Army initially engaged in successfully hijacking a plane bound for North Korea but eventually branched out to street violence, armed robbery, bombing, and assassinations.

Later, the group fractured into two smaller groups: One of them (led by Shigenobu Fusako) wanted to expand the international concern and reach of the group, especially in the Middle East, whereas the other (led by Moro Tsuneo) wanted to stay focused on Japan and Asia. The second of these two leaders (Tsuneo) later decided to conduct an internal terror campaign, kidnapping Red Army terrorists and beating some to death while leaving others to die, bound and gagged, in the wilderness. This terrorism—a type of internal purging—was meant not only to punish and visit retribution on those Army members out of step with the group's leadership but also to serve as a symbol of future terror—representing what would happen to other Red Army members who deviated from group leadership in this endeavor.[5] In many respects, the deaths of some Red Army members or the image of others left beaten, bound, and gagged in the wilderness served as a particularly potent threat.

## The Tupamaros

In Uruguay, a terrorist group known as the Tupamaros[6] practiced an effective decentralized terror campaign against government—and foreign—targets within the country.[7] According to the economist Arturo Porzecanski,[8] the Tupamaros felt that they could not force a successful revolution unless there was a unique intersection of political, social, and economic factors. This intersection, called the *coyuntura*, would provide a clarifying moment for all Uruguayans to see that revolution was necessary and that support for the Tupamaros was required. Terrorism was seen as a means of bringing on the *coyuntura*. The revolution—also known as the *salto*—against the government would come after this and would be waged by an army of the people. The acts of violence and destruction practiced by this group, which included arson, assassination, kidnapping, hijacking, and bank robbery, were, to some extent, engaged in for their symbolic worth. For example, spectacular daytime robberies of some of the country's largest banks (including one in which the Tupamaros took approximately $6 million) were meant to be symbolic of the image they wanted to create for themselves—that of Robin Hoods who would redistribute wealth to the people. Ultimately, however, this money was used only to finance their own operations, and the Tupamaros faced a public relations disaster with Uruguayans, who perceived them as little more than common thieves. To counter this impression, they later staged hijacking of food shipments, including one on Christmas Eve, with the food being redistributed to the poor and needy. The hijacking became a symbol of the public image they wanted—although by that point, many in the public were already skeptical about this as empty rhetoric.

## ❖ SYMBOLISM IN THE IMPLEMENTS AND TOOLS OF TERRORISM

Another productive source for study of symbolism and the act of terrorism can be found in the implements and tools of terror. Here I refer not as much to the act of violence and destruction as to the means by which the violence and destruction are enabled. What are the implements and tools of terror? These can include the specific kinds of weapons used, as well as the uniforms and propaganda tactics employed in a terrorist campaign.

### November 17

For example, a Greek terrorist group known as November 17 has waged a campaign against both Greek government and U.S./European imperialist targets for nearly 30 years. The origins for November 17 go back to opposition groups to the military junta in power in Greece from 1967 through 1974. This terrorist group took its name from a violent and tragic 1973 student uprising that helped to eventually fell the junta. It was and is the perception of those in November 17 that the junta only stayed in power for as long as it did because of the backing of the U.S. government. Consequently, even as the junta fell from power, November 17 turned its attentions to American targets, as well as others allied with the United States—especially those within NATO (the North Atlantic Treaty Organization). In that period of time, this group was responsible for numerous bombings and shootings, including 23 assassinations in Athens, starting in 1975 with then-CIA station chief Richard Welch. Of note for our purposes in the symbolism of implements and tools of terror is the fact that most of these assassinations were carried out with one of two .45 caliber handguns—a Browning or a Smith and Wesson, both of which could be identified (such that they became the group's calling cards), and both of which were made in America. This last point was most especially significant, as the members of this group wanted American targets to understand that they would be attacked with American weapons.[9] The handguns became symbols of violence by America being directed back at Americans.

### Terror From Above: The USSR and Afghanistan

In the period of time that the former Soviet Union suffered through its own kind of Vietnam experience, special forces troops in the employ of the Soviet state practiced a form of terrorism on Afghanis suspected of having ties to the warring Mujahadeen fighters. The Soviet Army, allegedly in Afghanistan at "the request" of the Afghani government (which itself had come to power after a coup in April 1978 with the full backing of the USSR), found itself in a rapidly worsening military conflict that would keep them there from December 1979 through February 1989—a decade!—at a cost of 15,000 Soviet soldiers (and those are only the ones in the official government accounting) and approximately 1 million Afghanis. Soviet troops employed a wide variety of conventional military weapons in Afghanistan, such as rocket launchers with Russian names like GRAD (translates to "hail") and URAGAN (translates to "hurricane"), large-caliber machine guns called DShKs, automatic rifles like the AK47 and the AK74, MIG and

SU fighter jets, and the enormous MI-18 and MI-24 helicopters, which could be used as flying gunships. As the United States had attempted in Vietnam, the Russian forces also attempted a form of psychological warfare in Afghanistan, designed to undermine popular support for the Mujahadeen.

One example of this Soviet-styled warfare—which would otherwise be called by its rightful name as state-sponsored terror *from above*—was the practice of concealing low-grade explosives in children's toys.[10] These toys were then dropped from the air (making this a literal terror from above) or left in villages suspected of sympathizing with the Mujahadeen. The purpose was for children to find and attempt to play with them before being killed or maimed by the explosive devices inside. The assumption was that the child might take the explosive-charged toy back to the area where the Mujahadeen were hiding and, when triggering the explosive, kill all within a certain blast radius. More often than not, however, children were the victims, and these toys became symbols of ruthless violence without conscience. The toys—like those children who were maimed but not killed—became symbols of lost innocence and senseless brutality. In either capacity, the goal had been to intimidate villagers and discourage them from assisting the Mujahadeen, but the opposite effect was achieved. The Mujahadeen, consistently outnumbered and underestimated by the Soviet military, became emboldened, even with heavy losses. The Soviet exodus from Afghanistan in 1989 could scarcely be called a triumph for the USSR.[11] Sadly, it is now alleged that the Russian Army has used this same tactic of explosives hidden within toys in its military conflict with Chechnya.[12]

## Suicide Bombers in Israel and Palestine

Similarly, in modern Israel and Palestine, the most recent violence in West Bank confrontations between Israeli settlers, Israeli military, and Palestinians living in areas ceded to the Palestinian Authority has created a trend toward a different kind of weapon—the so-called suicide bomber. Ironically, in this example, children, instead of becoming the target of toys that contain hidden bombs, become bombs themselves. Many young Palestinians—including in one instance, boys as young as 14 years old[13]—now feel compelled to become "human bombs," sacrificing themselves in the same terrorist act that then kills Israeli targets, both military and civilian. In this tragic and enduring conflict, which sometimes appears beyond political solution, the weapon of terror is combined with a human body, transforming the rhetorical symbolism in both. For some Israelis, the suicide bomber represents viciousness and inhumanity, but for many more, the suicide bomber is a symbol of the hopelessness and vulnerability of their situation—all in spite of vast military superiority and the backing of the United States. Regardless of all the security that comes with such advantages, Israelis are still forced to ask: How do you defend against this kind of terror without removing every possible suspect from the Israeli border? For many Palestinians, the suicide bomber becomes a symbol of heroism and martyrdom. They do not see this as an act of terror or murder so much as a kind of military response to Israeli occupation and denial of political freedom. And even for Palestinians who reject the concept of using this weapon against Israeli occupation, the symbolic power of the bomber as martyr makes it very difficult to openly criticize the act or the individual martyr. Worse for both sides, with the ongoing symbolic value of these bombers—admittedly different for both communities—there is little to suggest that the bombing will stop. If Israel makes concessions in the face of this terrorism, they will be perceived as legitimizing the efficacy of the terror—suggesting that it might make an effective weapon after all. There is no current political will to take any such stance in Israel today. Likewise, for Palestinians, this kind of terror becomes a response to occupation that guarantees carnage and headlines. It forces world attention—but maybe not always American sympathy—on their plight and condition. It may even become the instrument that, if impossible to respond to, results in diminished public confidence for those in power in Israeli government, maybe someday forcing a change in leadership.

## The Ku Klux Klan in America

The example of the Ku Klux Klan shows that the implements and tools of terrorism may also extend to the clothing of terrorists, as well as other artifacts in their possession. In the United States, the Klan has operated in various incarnations since 1867. I say *various incarnations* because it is often assumed that the KKK today is the same Klan that existed 135 years ago. In fact, organizationally, the Klan has had three different existences.

The Klan was initially conceived in the mid-1860s as a private club among six men in Tennessee, most of whom were college educated and had been officers in the Confederacy. As far as is known, their original purpose was not clearly defined, beyond enjoying dressing in costumes and riding between towns at night. The name they selected for themselves came from the ancient Greek word *kuklos,* which means "circle." They dressed as they imagined knights might have looked, and they remained a relatively secret club. They were more officially organized in 1867 under the leadership of Nathan Bedford Forrest. Forrest had been a respected and admired general of the defeated Confederate Army. According to some historical accounts, the original Klan was supposed to be composed of men like Forrest—ex-officers, wealthy and respected gentlemen who stood in opposition to suffrage for black Americans.[14] Forrest's tenure with the initial version of the Klan, however, lasted only a year or so, and he later resigned from its leadership and tried to disband the organization. By that point, however, membership in the Klan was filled with men who believed in violence of any kind—including assassination by shooting, stabbing, beating, or lynching, not to mention tarring, feathering, and whipping—to punish blacks and drive so-called Northern carpetbaggers from the South during the Reconstruction period immediately following the Civil War. During the next few years, the Klan was active in nine states, from Tennessee and the Carolinas to Mississippi, Texas, and Arkansas. Politically, the Klan was used as an organization in this period to control the black (at the time referred to as Negro) population, particularly with reference to suffrage.

In a fight between the federal Congress and the various state legislatures of many southern states, Democrats had been removed from power and replaced with so-called radical governments—usually made up of southerners who had been opposed to secession from the Union and who now embraced a form of suffrage for blacks. The real role of the Klan in this time was to undermine these new governments by attacking blacks and thinning the number of voters who might support the new regimes. By 1877, however, President Rutherford B. Hayes had withdrawn the last of his federal army from the South (there to enforce the terms of Reconstruction), and the pressure to oppose impositions from the North seemed to subside. There was still a considerable residue of hatred for the North, and plenty of vitriol for blacks still living in the South—but by this time, the perceived necessity for a Klan like what has been described was lessening.

A second incarnation of the Klan occurred in the 1920s, although the seeds for this new Klan had been sown some 15 years earlier. In

1905, Thomas Dixon published a best-selling book entitled *The Clansman*, which romanticized the earlier Klan that had fought against Reconstruction and presented its members as a kind of noble class striving to defend the civilized South in a post-Civil War period. In 1914, the rights for this book were sold to filmmaker D. W. Griffith, who then made a movie from the story (Griffith's version was, of course, the well-known *Birth of a Nation*), which "completed the process of rationalizing and romanticizing the Klan."[15] The positive reaction to the film helped create an environment within which the Klan could rise again, this time to be led by a 35-year-old veteran with a drinking problem and a checkered past in the Methodist Church: William Joseph Simmons. It was Simmons who actually created a new Klan, and with it a new organization. The newer incarnation of the Klan was almost like a fraternal organization such as the Masons— which, not coincidentally, had been in Simmons's background as well.

A new organization with the appearance of a fraternal organization, perhaps—but when it came to terrorism, the new Klan was the same old Klan, with the same kind of unchecked vigilantism that had featured in the Reconstruction period earlier. A slight difference in this second incarnation, however, was an expanded list of targets for the Klan, including Jews, Catholics, and immigrants of nonwhite European descent. Terrorism against these groups—especially the last of them— went largely unnoticed in this period because of public support for America's involvement in World War I. In fact, under Simmons, the new Klan even allied itself with the volunteer citizen-spying-on-citizen group called the Citizen's Bureau of Investigation.

Simmons later decided to improve the public image of the Klan by engaging the services of a public relations/advertising agency. As we shall discuss in greater detail in Chapter 6, this move helped construct the public face of the Klan and shaped public discourse about Klan activities of the time. By 1921, tens of thousands of eager recruits were signing up to join the Klan,[16] and by 1923, its membership was reported to be somewhere between 3 and 6 *million* people, with Klan chapters now in the northern and western United States as well as still in the South.[17] So pervasive was Klan influence in this period that it became politically acceptable to associate with the group, even for an American president. According to Wyn Craig Wade, even President Warren G. Harding entered the ranks of the Klan in a ceremony held in the White House.[18] By the end of the 1920s, however, and on the cusp of the Great Depression, the influence of the second Klan had again begun to wane.

Public tolerance for the group's violence and extremism had again subsided. By the end of the decade, Klan membership had again dropped, this time to barely 100,000. Through the next decade, Klan targets for their terrorism included the usual victims but also now communists (or socialists—Klan members seldom made the distinction) and unionists.

The third incarnation of the Klan really began with the U.S. Supreme Court decision of *Brown v. Board of Education,*[19] which declared segregation in public schools unconstitutional. Klan membership activity again increased, this time combining targets from the past with Jewish lawyers and allegedly communist judges who were seen as responsible for spurring the oncoming civil rights movement. In this last incarnation of the Klan, membership began to taper once more, and the Klan began making more alliances with white supremacy groups, some of which have lasted to this day.

Although each of these incarnations of the KKK has to some extent been shaped by its historical period, the eccentricities of its leadership, and the general tolerance (or lack thereof) of the public, there have been some consistencies throughout each period, most notably those that relate to symbolism and Klan artifacts.

From the time of the first Klan, members wore the distinctive white robes and hoods, initially claiming that these resembled the clothing of the much romanticized knights of an earlier period in European (and, really, British) history. What these original members of the Klan quickly discovered, however, was that the white uniforms had the effect—especially when worn at nighttime—of terrifying those who were the Klan's victims.[20]

At night, the robe and hood took on the appearance of ghostly apparitions, seemingly floating just above the ground or on horseback. And like the souls of legend that haunted the earth in the afterlife, these uniforms were symbols of death, serious injury, and destruction. Seeing them in the context of lynching, flogging, castration, shooting, stabbing, beating, and burning only reinforced this symbolism.

The same was true of a different Klan symbol: the burning cross. Members of the Klan (and even its own archivists) have long defended the use of the cross on religious grounds, asserting that the only symbolic value in this is the traditional one associated with Christianity. The records of Klan initiation and ritual tell a similar but mixed story. For example, in a document known as the *Kloran,*[21] also known as "The Book" (like a Bible) of the Invisible Empire, the ritual of the burning cross is explained in the following way. At a meeting (also called the *Kloncave*) of the Klan, the leader—the *Exalted Cyclops* (or EC, translated to mean a county commissioner)—will directly ask for a sacred altar to be prepared, with a Bible opened to Romans 12, and the altar flag of the Klan, along with a sword and a cross. Chapter 12, verse 21, of Romans reads, "Do not be conquered by evil, but conquer evil with good." The entire chapter actually addresses "the duties of a Christian," with focus upon sacrifice of the body and mind,[22] many parts but one body,[23] and mutual love.[24] All of this may seem somewhat misplaced in reference to the violent tendencies of the Klan, but it is intended to symbolize the relationship between a Klan member's responsibilities to the Klan and his society and the responsibilities of a Christian in addressing evil.

The cross is then ignited by a Klan officer called a *Klokard*, who addresses the EC and says, "Your excellency, the sacred altar of the Klan is prepared, the fiery cross illuminates the *Klavern*."

The EC is then to respond with these words: "Faithful Klokard, why the fiery cross?"

The Klokard replies: "Sir, it [the fiery cross] is the emblem of that sincere, unselfish devotion of all Klansmen, the sacred purpose and principles we have espoused."

The EC then says: "My Unit Leaders and Klansmen, what means the fiery cross?"

All assembled then reply in unison: "We serve and sacrifice for the right."[25]

Accordingly, the burning cross is intended to symbolize a connection between Christianity and the Klan, between Christian duties and Klan responsibilities, and between service and sacrifice.

What does the burning cross symbolize for those victims of the Klan's terrorism through the past 130-plus years? I have regularly put this question to my students in a law class dealing with the Constitution. For many African American students with familial roots in the South that go back at least one generation, the answer to my question will almost always be the same. What does the burning cross symbolize? In a word: lynching. The context of the symbol of terror provides one explanation for this.

The symbol of the burning cross means something quite different when placed in the context of the aforementioned violence and destruction. It was not uncommon for the burning cross to appear at a Klan gathering in the old South prior to a lynching.

Beyond context, one may also wish to reconsider the cross itself as a symbol. For Christians, it is a symbol of the resurrection, reinforcing the belief that Christ died and rose again in sacrifice for all who follow him. The cross itself, however, was in truth an instrument of torture and death. Crucifixion was intended as a means of capital punishment, with long and slow suffering before death—in a public display for all to see. Taken in the absence, for a moment, of the connection to the death and resurrection of Christ, the cross becomes a symbol of public execution. Adding the element of fire for a nighttime visit from the local Klan would only illuminate the symbol of the cross, again as a precursor to death.

## ❖  SYMBOLISM IN THE TARGET OF TERRORISM

The symbol in an act of terrorism may also be communicated in the specific target of the terror act. Whether by the terrorist's intent, or because of the meanings that a target audience consciously or subconsciously attaches to the target, the symbolic value may still be present and discoverable. To see how this works in practice, let us return to the example of the attack on the United States on September 11, 2001, and consider the choice of targets for the terrorism that ensued.

### Symbolism, the World
### Trade Center, and the Pentagon

In the time immediately following the attacks of September 11, much of the media and public attention focused upon the damage done to the World Trade Center (WTC) and specifically to the Twin Towers, which were the most significant components of the WTC complex. Of course, the WTC was only one of the targets struck on that fateful day. The Pentagon in Washington, D.C., was also a target, and it is believed that the White House or the Capitol Building was intended to be an additional target. In spite of this, most of our attention was drawn to New York. Why? The answer may have to do with the symbolism of the specific target in New York.

If we were to consider the WTC as a symbolic target, we might want to evaluate the intent of those who allegedly planned the attack. Why was the WTC targeted on September 11? Perhaps for no more complicated a reason than that it had been targeted in a bomb attack before.[26]

Maybe there was a sense of needing to complete an incomplete act, given that the prior bombing had caused loss of life and significant damage but nothing on a large scale. Or perhaps the WTC was targeted because the Twin Towers were two of the most recognizable buildings in the profile of New York—the sort of profile typically featured in photographs of the city. New York City is often regarded as a gateway to the United States from the East, and its diversity is often representative of all that is American. Damaging that profile and damaging the city was striking a blow against America—perhaps.

Or maybe the WTC was targeted because the towers were two of the largest buildings in the city and an attack there would be likely to cause more damage, loss of life, and injury than attacks on other targeted buildings. At the very least, with their incomparable height, the towers may have been targets because tall buildings are easier to hit with a plane.

The WTC had been the dream of the Rockefellers—David, then chairman of Chase Manhattan Bank, and Nelson, then governor of New York—who had wanted to name the two towers after themselves. New York City Mayor John Lindsay had insisted that the name for the entire complex be the World Trade Center. The buildings were designed by Japanese architect Minoura Yamasaki, who in the Twin Towers created what many felt was an overly orthodox, plain, and visually dull set of monolithic structures (for which many in the city initially criticized him). In addition to the towers, the WTC complex had five other, smaller office buildings. When completed, each tower had 110 stories, and the South Tower, 1,362 feet high, and the North Tower, 1,368 feet high, were the tallest buildings in the world at the time. The construction of Chicago's Sears Tower and Malaysia's Petronas Towers would eventually change that.

The WTC became home to many in the Western and global business community, not to mention specific American companies. Of all the businesses in the WTC, six banks, five investment firms, and three insurance companies had their headquarters there. The Bank of America had a significant presence there, and American Express occupied three floors. Both the Secret Service and the FBI had office space in the towers, as did 29 nations with trade missions and (ironically) virtually every major U.S. airline. In all, more than 50,000 people worked in the towers, and more than 200,000 tourists moved through all the buildings every day.

The World Trade Center thus was always busy, filled with activity and people. Would these factors explain the terrorists' fascination—perhaps preoccupation—with the WTC? In truth, this level of inquiry assumed that we could tell about the symbolic value of the targeting on September 11 by examining the terrorists' intent. But even after our war in Afghanistan, and even after all the incarceration, "debriefing," and questioning of former Taliban and al Qaeda personnel, we have little hard evidence of the exact intentions for these specific targets—and especially for the WTC.

Forgetting the terrorists' motives at this point, would the above factors in background of the WTC explain our own fixation with the target site after September 11? Not necessarily. The Pentagon is also a significant and well-known structure, and on that date it, too, was struck and significantly damaged, also with loss of life. Possibly more horrible was the fate of those passengers on United Flight 93, which crashed in Shanksville, Pennsylvania, only after courageous passengers, made aware of their impending doom, charged the cockpit in an attempt to take control of the plane. We assume today that the crashed jet was targeting Washington, D.C., and either the White House or the Capitol Building. As we wrestle in our own minds with the fears and anxiety of being attacked anywhere and any time, can any of us imagine the horror of learning that our plane has been hijacked, and later learning that it will be used as a weapon to destroy a large building and kill many people besides those in the plane? In short, there were many horrors on that date, and though New York's tragedy may certainly have been on a larger scale, with greater loss of life and damage, the loss was relative. The Pentagon was an equally significant target, and the suffering of those victims in the WTC was surely no greater or more horrific than that of the passengers on the flight that crashed in Pennsylvania. So what is it about New York and the Twin Towers that was and is different?

Perhaps the answer to this question—and an answer to why the WTC was targeted in the first place—can be found in the rhetorical significance of the structures. Many have proclaimed architecture as rhetoric before,[27] whether comparing buildings and structures,[28] amusement and theme parks,[29] or even memorial structures and meaning.[30] Nowhere is this rhetorical dimension of architecture more pronounced than in the division of modernist architecture and postmodern architecture. Modernist architecture—which can be seen in structures like public housing projects or tall business buildings like skyscrapers—symbolizes both rejection of classical and historical thought and celebration of "twentieth century's achievements and dominance of technological innovation, rationality and corporate power."[31] Modernist architecture has focused less on form or aesthetic style and more on function, efficiency, and order—not unlike that philosophy around which corporate business was organized and developed in this past century.[32] Thus, modernist architecture is often simple, with relatively clean lines for design and much forethought devoted to that which is functional and rational—even if boring and dull.

Postmodern architecture, by contrast, is often seen as a reaction to modernist architecture. With design styles that defy a definable or universal standard or genre, the postmodern architectural style is more easily identified by its rejection of modernity; implicitly, therefore, it is a rejection of rationality, technology, and corporatism. Design styles in postmodern architecture do not celebrate simplicity, symmetry, efficiency, or function as ends unto themselves or goals toward which our society should aim. Postmodern architecture—which can be seen in examples like the Vietnam Veterans' Memorial in Washington, D.C., or San Francisco's relatively new Museum of Modern Art—suggests that architecture must be considered in relation to other structures as well as the general environment and that a building or structure must be evaluated as "part of a cultural and physical context."[33] The postmodern architecture must interact with others in that context. In these ways, postmodern architecture must be viewed as inherently political.[34]

Seen in this light, the WTC generally and the Twin Towers specifically may be considered as clear examples of modernist architecture. The towers were, as previously referenced, relatively simple and dull monolithic structures. They were, as the name of the complex (World *Trade* Center) ultimately suggested, and as the list of building occupants clearly demonstrated, celebrations of corporatism on both an American and a global scale.

Am I suggesting here that the towers were targeted because they were symbolic examples of modernity? Not entirely. Or am I suggesting that our fascination and concern with them as a target of terrorism represents a public concern with terrorism targeting modernity? Again, the answer is no. Words like *modernism* and *postmodernism* are mostly used by academics (and not even then do all of the users understand the terms entirely!). What I would claim, however, is that the symbolic value of the Twin Towers changed on the day of September 11 and that the towers moved from being examples of the modern in structure to examples of the postmodern in the moment of their destruction—and that in that way, the terrorist attack on these symbols was inherently rhetorical. The *destruction* of these buildings was a *deconstruction* of their symbolic meaning and a subsequent rearrangement of a new symbol that had serious political meaning for the United States.

To understand this, let us refine our explanation of the Twin Towers as examples of modernist architecture and also consider them as symbols of something else. In simple, visual form, the Twin Towers stood out because they were big and tall—but, most important, because they were towers plural and not a tower in the singular sense. There were two of them, and although the North Tower was a few feet taller than the South, they were for the most part identical from the outside. In that way, they resembled not so much identical towers as they did posts to a fence, or perhaps a gate.

If we were for the moment to consider the other targets of terrorism on that day, we might discover that they, too, formed symbolic components of a fence or wall, metaphorically speaking, surrounding and (falsely perhaps) insulating the United States from the rest of the world. The Pentagon, for example, could be considered symbolic of the military might behind the United States, without which we might not be the one remaining and undisputed global superpower in the world.

Likewise, the White House and the Capitol Building are symbolic of our political strength at the national level, without which, again, we would not be considered a global superpower. Indeed, reconsidered in this way, the towers themselves were symbols of corporatism—and in that way, of the third leg of the real American triad—economic strength. Without economic strength, the United States would be no better than Russia (still armed to the teeth but with only a developing economy and still emerging political control).

The symbolism of each target on that day makes more sense when you consider each target in relation to one other. In context, all were symbols of the strength (or veneer of strength) behind American superiority. By attacking these symbols, terrorists on that day undermined the value of this strength, causing us all to reconsider our role in the world, not to mention our individual security.

Conceptualizing the towers as the gateposts to this wall (military, economic, political), securing our country makes more sense if we also consider that a gatepost controls both the entrance and the exit to a place. Our economy is likewise the most accessible point of origin for our society. The concept of "the American Dream" rests upon the idea that people from anywhere can come to the United States and, within a generation, improve their standard of living. For those who come to this country, the gate of economic opportunity—a central strength of our country—allows access.

Like the gateposts of mythology involving castles—or the city/states enclosed by walls—the Twin Towers were symbolic not only of our economic strength but also of our insulation and protection. Though our economy was and is accessible, it is still protected by laws and customs favoring American business and culture, reinforcing our dominant economic position in the world. In the gatepost towers of any castle or city/state, the towers themselves had to represent the tallest and most structurally sound portion of the wall barrier in order to guarantee the integrity of the gate.

In Homer's mythological description of the fall of Troy, it was not until Greek soldiers led by Odysseus and hidden within the fabled Trojan Horse were brought into the city/state and revealed themselves in a surprise attack on the city that the gate was opened for the larger Greek invasion and destruction of the same.[35] When our towers collapsed following the attack of September 11, it was as if the gate had been crushed and forced open and the soundness of our impregnable position exposed. In that way, the meaning of the symbol changed, from one celebrating modernity and the triumph of corporatism in our economic strength to something else entirely. In that pile of rubble and debris later known as *Ground Zero* (yet another rhetorical labeling) was a new symbol of our vulnerability.

## ❖ SUMMARY

Terrorism as an act of violence and destruction can also be understood by the symbolic value attached to the terror act. When we describe something as a symbol, or declare that it possesses symbolic value, we are suggesting that this thing—whether an object, a word, a sound, or conduct—may be interpreted to mean something more than itself. All nonverbal acts are to some degree expressive and thus inherently symbolic. By employing communication tools looking for the intent of the actor, the context of the situation, and the relativity of the message, we may discover what that symbolic meaning is.

In terrorism, we have seen that symbolism may be found in the act of violence and destruction itself, in the implements and tools of terror, or even in the specific targets of the terror act—all of which significantly contribute to the manner in which we construct what terrorism means for us. In this next chapter, we consider how our public discourse about this meaning is further affected and (if we aren't careful) manipulated by official rhetoric that can be found in speeches by political leaders.

## ❖ NOTES

1. See *United States v. O'Brien*, 391 U.S. 367 (1968), wherein the Court acknowledged as much but was loath to extend First Amendment protection to every kind of nonverbal action. See also *Spence v. Washington*, 418 U.S. 495 (1974), in which the Court fashioned a legal test to determine when nonverbal conduct might be considered expressive within the meaning of free speech under the First Amendment. The Court's model here, called the "expressive conduct test," is still in use today.

2. Philip Emmert and Victoria J. Lukasko, *Interpersonal Communication* (New York: William Brown, 1984), p. 47.

3. See, e.g., Steven W. Littlejohn, *Theories of Human Communication* (Belmont, CA: Wadsworth, 1983), pp. 5–7; see also Douglas M. Fraleigh and Joseph S. Tuman, *Freedom of Speech in the Marketplace of Ideas* (New York: St. Martin's Press, 1997), 281–82.

4. James Gilligan, *Violence: Our Deadly Epidemic and Its Causes* (New York: Putnam Books, 1996), p. 61.

5. For more about the Japanese Red Army, see William R. Farrell, *Blood and Rage: The Story of the Japanese Red Army* (Lexington, MA: Lexington Books, 1990).

6. Initially, this group, run by a disillusioned law student named Raul Sendic, aimed at social revolution, government reform, and the creation of economic opportunities. In 1963, the group's official name was the National Liberation Movement (MLN), but over time, the group embraced violence as a means for social change and felt the need to have a name with more popular appeal, as well as one that would connect their violent means to a historic context. They settled on the name Tupamaros, after the heroic Inca chieftain Tupac Amuru. Amuru had been killed in a revolt against Spanish conquerors 200 years before.

7. John B. Wolf, *Fear of Fear* (New York: Plenum, 1981), p. 82.

8. Arturo C. Porzecanski, *Uruguay's Tupamaros* (New York: Praeger, 1973).

9. Significant results in breaking up this group have only recently been achieved, as of summer 2002, with the assistance of the Greek government and law enforcement. Some have speculated, however, that this cooperation from Greek officials came about only because of the prospect of the Athens Olympics in 2004 and a desire to alleviate pressure from influential participant nations such as the United States. For more, see Anthee Carassava, "Greeks Claim a Victory Against a Small Band of Political Assassins," *New York Times*, July 19, 2002, p. A3.

10. For more, see Michael Elliot, "Down and Dirty," *Time*, October 14, 2002, retrieved from Time Magazine Web site: www.TIME.com.

11. For more on the USSR military campaign in Afghanistan, see Vladimir Tamarov, *Afghanistan: A Russian Soldier's Story* (Berkeley: Ten Speed Press, 2001).

12. See staff article for "Powerless to Act? Not So: The West Cannot Ignore Its Duty to Chechnya," *Guardian*, November 6, 1999, retrieved from www.cdi.org/russia/johnson/3609.HTML.

13. David Rohde, "Passions Inflamed, Gaza Teenagers Die in Suicidal Attacks," *New York Times*, June 25, 2001, pp. A1, A15.

14. Thomas Gossett, *Race: The History of an Idea in America* (New York: Oxford University Press, 1997), pp. 258–61.

15. Shawn Lay, "Introduction: The Second Invisible Empire," in *The Invisible Empire in the West: Toward a Historical Reappraisal of the Ku Klux Klan of the 1920s*, ed. Shawn Lay (Urbana: University of Illinois Press, 1992), p. 4.

16. Ibid., p. 7.

17. Gossett, *Race*, p. 371.

18. Wyn Craig Wade, *Fiery Cross: The Ku Klux Klan in America* (New York: Simon and Schuster, 1987), p. 165.

19. 347 U.S. 483, 74 S.Ct. 686, 98 L.Ed. 873 (1954).

20. John Hope Franklin, *From Slavery to Freedom* (New York: Knopf, 2000); see also Gossett, *Race*, p. 260.

21. It is not clear if this pun was intentional or the result of putting the "Kl" in front of as many words as Klan members do (e.g., they meet at a *Klonklave*, and the meeting is called to order by a *Klaliff*), but here the word *Kloran* is similar in appearance to another recognizable holy book—the Koran.

22. Rom. 12:1–2.

23. Rom. 12:3–8.

24. Rom. 12: 9–21.

25. For a complete text of the Kloran, see W. H. Weller, *Under the Hood: Unmasking the Modern Ku Klux Klan* (North Manchester, IN: DeWitt Books, 1998), pp. 127–48.

26. The original bombing occurred in 1993. Using some 1,300 pounds of explosives placed in the garage, terrorists killed six people and injured approximately 1,000 more.

27. See, e.g., Umberto Eco, "Function and Sign: The Semiotics of Architecture," in *Signs, Symbols and Architecture*, ed. Geoffrey Broadbent, Richard Bunt, and Charles Jencks (New York: John Wiley, 1980), pp. 11–69.

28. See, e.g., Darryl Hattenhauer, "The Rhetoric of Architecture: A Semiotic Approach," *Communication Quarterly* 32 (1984): 71–77.

29. See, e.g., Elizabeth Walker Mechling and Jay Mechling, "The Sale of Two Cities: A Semiotic Comparison of Disneyland With Marriot's Great America," *Journal of Popular Culture* 37 (1973): 253–63.

30. See, e.g., Carole Blair, Marsha S. Jeppeson, and Enrico Pucci, Jr., "Public Memorializing in Post-Modernity: The Vietnam Veterans Memorial as Prototype," *Quarterly Journal of Speech* 77 (1991): 289–308.

31. Ibid., p. 291.

32. Steven Connor, *Postmodern Culture: An Introduction to Theories of the Contemporary* (Oxford, England: Basil Blackwell Press, 1989), p. 76.

33. Robert Stern, "The Doubles of Post-Modern," *Harvard Architectural Review* 1 (1980): 75–87.

34. Blair et al., "Public Memorializing," p. 292.

35. Homer, *The Odyssey of Homer*, trans. Richmond Lattimore (New York: Harper Perennial, 1991), 4.271–89, 8.499–520, and 9.523–37.

# 5

# Public Oratory About
# Terrorism

In Chapter 3, we briefly reviewed the development of rhetoric, some of which centered on the contribution of the ancient Greeks and the schism between the Sophists and, later, Plato and Aristotle, the latter of whom felt that public speaking and rhetoric were less ends unto themselves and more the sine qua non of good citizenship. In developing a modern theory of rhetoric, we also referenced neoclassical theory, the contemporary application of Aristotle's ideas about oratory and persuasion. In this chapter, we will examine the relationship between public oratory and the general discourse we have concerning terrorism and how we construct its meaning—or how that meaning is constructed for us. By *public oratory,* I am referring not just to any speeches made on the subject of terrorism but to those speeches for a public audience, made by our leaders or those of other countries, decision makers, individuals in authority, and those most likely to shape public opinion. Naturally, I could be referring to any senior member of government (e.g., in this country, a president or a Secretary of State); a former authority figure (e.g., a former leader like President Clinton); an expert recognized by the public (e.g., a well-known academic whose advice is relied upon by people in government); and so on. In the interest of space and economy, however, I will here focus on only one speaker—a sitting president—whose speeches on terrorism should be well known to the reader at this time.

In this chapter, we will look at two speeches given by President George W. Bush in response to terrorism and the events of September 11. As leaders and authority figures, presidents occupy unique positions in American and global politics. A sitting president is the leader of our country but, by the rules of our Constitution, must share political power with the legislative branch of government (the Congress), and both the president and the Congress must have that power checked by the judicial branch of government (hence the old concept of *checks and balances*). Nevertheless, the president enters the game of shared power with considerable resources at his (and someday her) disposal—one of which concerns the single voice with which he speaks on foreign affairs. It has been our custom throughout the history of our country to allow the president to speak with one voice for all of us in matters of foreign affairs. It is true that Congress, controlling appropriations (i.e., the money to pay for things) still has influence in matters of foreign affairs and that the federal judiciary (and most especially the Supreme Court) will ensure that nothing a president does even in the foreign arena blatantly violates our Constitution—but these facts notwithstanding, foreign affairs are still the president's domain. This authority is bolstered by the fact that the Department of State is folded under the executive branch of government, as well as the fact that the president has the title of commander-in-chief of all the armed forces. In times of foreign conflict—especially involving war or the threat of war—the president's authority is unmatched. Even though our Congress passed a law called the War Powers Act[1] after our conflict in Vietnam, requiring more of a role for the Senate in the making of war, the act was filled with loopholes and is today a post facto measure, for the Senate does not get involved until after the fact, and only if the president formally declares war or has committed American troops for combat beyond a certain statutory period.[2] Smart presidents since that time have been loath to declare war (although in some crises, their rhetoric comes awfully close to *sounding* like a declaration of war) and have also been careful about time periods for deployment of troops, or what language they would use in describing the reasons for sending troops in the first place. The result has been that the president acts and speaks for us in a relatively unchecked, single-minded manner. For all of these reasons, presidents make ideal subjects for studying the effects of public oratory on matters of public concern—especially a topic like terrorism, which, when committed on American soil, has the feel of war declared on America. Although here I will focus our examination on two of the more rhetorically significant addresses given by President George W. Bush in the aftermath of the terrorist attacks on September 11, let me stress that there are many acts of terror against this country and others (both *terror from above* and *from below*) that could be evaluated in the context of the public oratory they incite and how those shape discourse. I have elected in this chapter to use only these two examples because of time and space constraints.

Before I come to any discussion of the two speeches, however, I think it is important to first return to the mention of rhetoric—our rhetorical strand for this aspect of terrorism as a communication process—and address how we evaluate public oratory to discover its rhetorical function.

## ❖ A METHOD OF RHETORIC FOR PUBLIC ORATORY

Using the notion of neoclassical theory as a springboard, I will suggest the following methodology in this section, first by examining the notion of rhetoric, public speaking, and persuasion as being *audience centered,* then by examining the development of specific *rhetorical appeals* to affect that persuasion, and finally by considering how these appeals translate into actual persuasive messages with the assistance of *rhetorical figures* of speech and with the occasional use of *rhetorical fallacies.* Let's consider each of these in turn.

### Public Speaking and Persuasion as Audience-Centered Rhetoric

Although it would seem that any discussion of this subject (especially one employing a modern application of Aristotle's ideas) should begin with an examination of appeals in the speech message proper, I feel that this puts the cart before the horse. In truth, effective public speaking and persuasion recognizes that its rhetoric must be created for and targeted to a specific audience (or audiences). Before we can talk about the persuasive message itself, therefore, we have to begin our discussion by understanding what and who the audience is, because considerations of audience drive the creation of effective persuasive messages in the first place. Of necessity, we must begin our discussion of methodology with a comment about the significance of audience and how it is analyzed by the speaker/rhetor before the creation of the message. By understanding how and why speechwriters and speakers (not always the same person) make assumptions about audience, we can begin the process of deconstructing a public speech to understand how it works its influence on the intended audience. How does the creator of the speech message make assumptions about his or her audience?

The first question that must be asked is: *Who is the specific audience for this speech?*[3] On occasion, there will be only one audience—but in truth, for most public speeches like the kind given by a president, there will be multiple audiences. These may include (but are not limited to) members of the president's own party, or those of the opposition party; they may include all of the members of the armed forces—the Army, Navy, Air Force, Marines, Coast Guard, and so on—or members of the White House and the executive branch, or members of the Congress; they may include foreign governments of countries who are our allies, or those who are neutral to the interests of the United States, or even our supposed enemies; they may also include any and/or all of the residents of those countries on whose support the leadership of their governments depend. Audiences may include important captains of industry in our business sectors, or important bankers and investment officials who need to be comforted or reassured by the president's words. They may include the leaders of state governments, or state and local law enforcement personnel, whose cooperation the president may require for an initiative. Audiences may also include lobbyists and the leaders of special interest groups who regularly contribute money and resources to campaigns for politicians who support their positions, while campaigning vigorously against those who oppose them. Most fundamentally, audiences may obviously include the American people—regardless of party affiliation—whose interests the president is supposed to represent and serve and upon whose good graces a reelection bid may hang.

Understanding more about who the audience is can be facilitated by asking questions about *audience demographics*[4] (e.g., age, race, ethnicity, cultural background, religion, education, political orientation); *size of the audience*[5] (how many people will be in the audience); *when the speech will be seen by the audience*[6] (both for those in attendance and for those who may be watching on television, listening on radio, or doing either on the Internet); *how much time will be allotted for the speech*[7] (i.e., for how long can one speak to the audience); and *where the speech will take place*[8] (i.e., questions about forum, which are most relevant for a live audience but can play a role when the event is witnessed on television and the location creates a sense of background scenery/ context for the speech).

Next, the creator of the speech may inquire: *Is there any possibility for common ground between the speaker/rhetor and the audience?*[9] In practice, this means considering whether there is anything in the background or situation of the audience that may also be found in the background or situation of the speaker. For example, if the president was addressing a group of concerned parents about the problems of teenage drinking, he might make reference to the challenges he has faced as a parent concerned with alcohol use by his own teenage daughters. So doing suggests that a common ground or bond exists between the speaker and the audience—that he understands their concerns or situation because these are his concerns or his situation too.

Another audience-centered question the creator of the speech may ask is: *Has the audience heard the speech message before?*[10] This is also known as "prior exposure to the message," and it deals with whether the audience has already been exposed to the speech message and formed some kind of opinion or position in response. Has the audience heard this before? If so, what was the reaction? Was it what the speaker wanted? If it was a negative reaction, why did this happen? Surprisingly, some speakers are foolish about repeating speech messages that have proven unpopular or ineffective with audience members in the past. Sometimes, speakers do this because they are dogmatic and stubborn about their own positions; other times, they do this because they failed to consider the audience and prior exposure. In either event, it is a general rule of crafting speeches for specific audiences that what has worked in the past rhetorically will work again in the future, assuming that conditions and circumstances for the audience have not changed. For example, the senior George Bush, former president of the United States, decided to emphasize a traditional message in his speeches for election in the campaign of 1988. These included references to themes that his predecessor President Reagan had evoked in the previous campaigns of 1980 and 1984, such as a need for strong defense, decreasing the tax burden, diminishing the role of the federal government in the private life of a citizen (or a business!), and return of greater political power to states and localities. It made sense for Bush, a former vice president under a popular president in Reagan, to repeat these same ideas in his speech messages in 1988. Of course, by 1992, conditions and circumstances had changed. How? The Soviet Union had broken up, and the Berlin Wall had crumbled. The concept of a political enemy in the Soviet communists was a strong rationale in much of the rhetoric used to advocate a stronger defense and more military spending. But by 1992, that rationale wasn't effective for most voters because the old enemy no longer existed. In its place were new defense concerns, but President Bush's rhetoric never really effectively defined these in a way that resonated with voters. At the same time, he was accused—even by members of his own party—of going back on a pledge to never raise taxes. And of course, in that election year, the economy was still in recession, and many people felt vulnerable, while others suffered hardship from the downturn of events. Taken with that set of changed conditions and circumstances for the targeted audience of his reelection speeches in 1992, it is not hard to understand why Bush failed to connect with voters. Though it is true that messages that are effective can be repeated, it is also true that those messages should not be repeated if conditions and circumstances have changed the audience's disposition about the message. What worked for the senior Bush in 1988 was exactly what proved to be his undoing in 1992.

A final audience-centered question the creator of the speech message may wish to consider is: *What is the disposition of the audience to the speech message, or to the speaker on a personal level?*[11] Here we would look to see if there was any evidence of audience disposition to be discovered from the other aspects of audience analysis we have discussed so far. How will the audience feel about the message the speaker is presenting? What is its disposition toward the speaker on a personal basis? In contemporary practice, we think of broad classifications to describe audience orientation to the message or speaker. These include classifying all or part of an audience as *hostile* to the message or speaker (meaning that audience members cannot be persuaded because they are so opposed to what is being said or to the speaker personally); *sympathetic* (meaning that they are, in effect, already persuaded because of their support, love, adoration, agreement, etc., with the message or speaker from previous experience); or *neutral* (meaning that no firm disposition exists toward speaker or message—the audience is yet to be persuaded). Though it is possible in theory for an entire audience to be classified as one or the other of these, more commonly—especially for public speeches delivered by presidents—elements of all three classifications may be found in the audience. Or to put this a different way, it is more likely that for most presidential addresses, there will be multiple audiences, which are divided along the lines of hostility, sympathy, or neutrality. Knowing this ahead of time helps the creator of the message to know what message is intended for what audience; likewise, it helps us to understand, when we deconstruct a speech, why certain message choices were made.

## Public Speaking, Oratory, and Rhetorical Appeals

Now that we have considered the audience, the next part of our methodology for public oratory is to consider the message itself. Here we may reach back to Chapter 2 and our discussion of Aristotle and entertain three concepts he introduced in developing a theory of rhetoric. These concepts are still in use today by neoclassical theorists. They are the concepts of a persuasive speech message, classified as ethos, pathos, and logos. Of course, their effectiveness will depend on the audience; we are not all affected by ethos, pathos, and logos in the same ways.

In contemporary application, *ethos* refers to credibility—and specifically to the credibility of the speaker or rhetor, the messenger. When we say that a speech message is imbued with a strong sense of ethos, we are suggesting that the speaker him- or herself has a strong sense of credibility with the given audience. Of course, credibility can take many forms. For example, an individual may be credible because he or she is an *authority figure* (a person of power and responsibility), like a political leader. Or a person may be credible because he or she is an *expert* on the subject addressed, like a scientist or a researcher. Or an individual may be deemed credible because he or she has *experience* with the subject he or she discusses—like Christopher Reeve, who, though not a medical expert on the subject of broken spines and paralysis, can still speak effectively because of his own experience. Perhaps an individual may be found credible because he or she is trustworthy and honest, such as someone in whom you really trust and believe. (Can you think of any people like this? How about a close friend or family member?) If an individual possesses some amount of ethos, we may say that he or she will be effective with the audience not necessarily because the speech message content itself is effective and persuasive but more because the speaker him- or herself is credible. A powerful leader like the president will often have the ethos of credibility that comes from authority, but since the Watergate era, that has not always guaranteed that audiences would automatically believe anything a president had to say. Different presidents since that time have affected different forms of rhetorical ethos. For example, President Carter, though not perceived as an effective leader by the end of his administration, was nevertheless perceived to be an intelligent man, and a very honest one, a perception confirmed in 2002 when he was awarded the Nobel Peace Prize. In contrast, President Reagan, Carter's successor, was a highly popular and likable leader, with an ethos that touched even his political opponents. Though many Democrats may have opposed Reagan's policies, most would still admit they liked him on a personal level. The American people were no different; though many disagreed with Reagan's positions on issues like abortion or separation of church and state, they still liked him on a personal level and could be persuaded to vote for him. President Clinton, like President Reagan, was also an immensely popular leader—even to the point where his public support remained unflinchingly solid in the face of impeachment over whether he had perjured himself in an investigation over an alleged affair with Monica Lewinsky. Clinton's ethos, however, was different from Reagan's. How would we describe this ethos? Whereas both men shared enormous charisma, Clinton was often perceived as credible for his intelligence and command of detail, while Reagan—the so-called Teflon President—was more like a general or corporate CEO. Acting above the level of detail for which Clinton was known, President Reagan was seen as an authority figure who could see the big picture and make the larger decision.

A second form of rhetorical appeal identified for us by Aristotle is what he called *pathos,* or the appeal of emotion. Here we are describing speech rhetoric that persuades and affects an audience because it appeals to them on an emotional level. Not surprisingly, much of the rhetoric employed by presidents in their speeches to different audiences employs pathos-centered appeals. For example, President Clinton, speaking in the aftermath of the violent tragedy at Columbine High School, made reference to the deaths of so many young people to make a larger point about the need for gun control. Though the president's point may have been logically connected to the gun control argument, the first way it hit many in the nation was emotionally because the memory of so many young victims was present in our consciousness.

Likewise, when the senior President Bush chose to make flag burning a political issue for the campaign in 1988, he employed rhetoric suggesting that support for the physical symbol of the flag was in some way a litmus test for an individual's patriotism to this country. Anyone who dared to support flag burning was unpatriotic and un-American. Ironically, a year later, the U.S. Supreme Court declared that burning the flag was symbolic, political expression, protected by the First Amendment.[12] It would not have been difficult for the senior Bush to have explained his argument in logical terms,[13] but he instead made this a mostly emotional argument involving the aforementioned patriotism.

A third form of rhetorical appeal identified for us by Aristotle is *logos*—the appeal of logic or reasoning. In contemporary terms, we are describing rhetoric that succeeds with an audience because the message is rational and logical. There are many different ways to use logos appeals, but the kind with which you may be most familiar involves the use of *deductive reasoning*. This form of reasoning operates from the assumption that if certain statements—called argumentative premises—are true, then a certain conclusion must follow. If you have already enjoyed a class in critical thinking, you will undoubtedly have been exposed to this kind of argument before—usually in the form of what is called a *syllogism*. With a syllogism, there are two premises, the major premise and the minor premise that must be true if a certain argumentative conclusion is to follow. For example, you may recall this syllogism from a class in critical thinking:

*Major Premise:* All men are mortal.

*Minor Premise:* Socrates is a man.

*Conclusion:* Socrates is mortal.

Note that when this kind of appeal is used in oratory, the speaker seldom (if ever) uses language to suggest that something is a "major premise" or a "minor premise." More often, we find these premises embedded in the text of the speaker's arguments as we deconstruct them.

Presidents, when trying to make a case to a certain audience, will sometimes use logos-based appeals with deductive reasoning in their speeches. More often, however, the use of these appeals must be kept relatively simple because the audience(s) for the president will be diverse and not always capable of understanding a complex argument in the same way. In such situations (which are common for speaker/rhetors addressing large audiences), simple is better!

For example, it was, ironically, former President Richard Nixon—someone who had the ethos of a fighter and a staunch anticommunist—who later argued that negotiation with Communist China would not be possible without first improving relations with the country. His symbolic visit to China (the first by an American president since the communist revolution there) was the culmination of an argument he had already made to the Congress and the country. The premises for this were relatively simple. Peaceful coexistence (and containment) of China required negotiation between our countries. Negotiation between the two countries, in turn, required normal relations. Therefore, it followed that peaceful coexistence with China would flow from normalizing relations. The more complex realities of using our improved relations with China to help drive a dividing wedge in the damaged relationship between China and the Soviet Union made for more complexity than Nixon wanted to convey.

If he is to be effective, a president's decision to employ one or more of these appeals is ultimately driven by the assumptions he (or the speechwriters) makes about the audiences being addressed. As indicated before, not every appeal works with every audience member in the same way—if at all. Accordingly, it is rarely the case that a president's rhetoric reflects only *one* of these kinds of appeals. More commonly, there will be a blend of two or perhaps all three of the appeals, depending on the audience analysis that has already been conducted. Later in this chapter, I will discuss how these appeals are used in presidential rhetoric about terrorism; for the time, what would you assume would be the most common form of appeal to employ when discussing terrorism before the American people?

### Public Speaking, Oratory, and Rhetorical Figures

Understanding whether the speech message is ethos, pathos, or logos oriented for the specific audience(s) is an important step to deconstructing the public oratory of individuals like our political leaders—especially on topics like terrorism. The next step is to examine how these messages are actually worded to create the desired rhetorical effect. To appreciate this, we will here consider how *rhetorical figures of speech and argument* are used. Rhetorical figures are the actual techniques for wording specific kinds of claims and arguments, and although there are literally hundreds of these, I will (for the sake of space considerations) focus on those that are most relevant to our discussion about presidential orations. These include accumulation, anaphora, antithesis, catalogue, personification, and prolepsis.

The first of these, *accumulation,* refers to a situation in which two or more clauses are used in succession within a speech, saying essentially the same thing. This is often done for emphasis and/or clarity. For example, during the 1960 presidential election, questions were raised about the fact that candidate John F. Kennedy was a Catholic, with some charging that his election would be dangerous for the United States because his first allegiance on different issues might be to whatever the Vatican's positions were. Answering this charge with an eloquent speech,[14] Kennedy used accumulation when he said:

I am wholly opposed to the state being used by *any religious group, Catholic or Protestant, to compel, prohibit, or persecute the free exercise of any other religion. And that goes for any persecution at any time, by anyone, in any country* (emphasis added to show accumulation).[15]

Here "religious groups," and "Catholics and Protestants" are saying essentially the same thing. The same is true for "compel, prohibit, or persecute," and "at any time, by anyone, in any country."

By contrast, another figure called *anaphora* deals with the repetition of a word or phrase at the beginning of successive phrases, clauses, or lines. Like accumulation, this is often done for emphasis and clarity— as well as for sense of rhetorical style. For example, Lyndon Baines Johnson, who was sworn into office as president with the assassination of President Kennedy, addressed a joint session of Congress shortly thereafter,[16] in which he said:

All I have I would have given gladly not to be standing here today. The greatest leader of our time has been struck down by the foulest deed of our time. Today, John Fitzgerald Kennedy lives on in the immortal words and works that he left behind. *He lives on* in the minds and memories of mankind. *He lives on* in the hearts of his countrymen (emphasis added to show anaphora).

The repetition of the words "he lives on" allows Johnson to emphasize Kennedy's memory and creates a sense of style for the pathos-oriented speech to multiple audiences.

A third rhetorical figure, called *antithesis,* deals with clauses in a speech set in opposition to one another, usually to distinguish between choices, concepts, and ideas. For example, in his first inaugural address,[17] President Richard Nixon closed his speech with antithesis, encouraging his audience to remember that "our destiny offers *not the cup of despair, but the chalice of opportunity"* (emphasis added to show antithesis). Here, Nixon sets the "cup of despair" in opposition to the "chalice of opportunity," leaving his large audience with a clear choice (after all, who would opt for despair over opportunity?) in this speech with mixed pathos and logos, along with the ethos of the presidency as an authority source.

A fourth example of a figure for our review is *catalogue,* in which a speaker/rhetor offers a list of things, ideas, or arguments. Often this is done in conjunction with a logos appeal to suggest evidence or support for a claim the speaker is making. Beyond making the message appear logical, this figure may also strengthen a speaker/rhetor's ethos as expert and trustworthy source by making the speaker appear as if he or she has considered all the possibilities. Political leaders often make use of this device. For example, former President Gerald Ford, in a speech[18] to a joint session of Congress, explained his vision for a new energy policy to cure the nation's energy problems.

America's future depends heavily on oil, gas, coal, electricity, and other resources called energy. Make no mistake, we have an energy problem. The primary solution has to be at home. . . . I have ordered today the *reorganization of our national energy effort* and the *creation of a national energy board.* It will be charged with developing a *single national energy program.* . . . *New legislation* will be sought after your recess to require use of *cleaner coal processes* and *nuclear fuel in new electric plants,* and the *quick conversion of existing oil plants.* . . . I will use the *Defense Production Act to allocate scarce materials for energy development.* . . . I will *meet with top management of the automobile industry* to assure . . . a firm *program* aimed at *achieving a forty percent increase in gas mileage* within a 4-year deadline (emphasis added to illustrate catalogue).[19]

Here, Ford lists aspects of his energy effort and program. The sum total of this list of initiatives is designed to rhetorically suggest that Ford is actively trying to lead by comprehensively dealing with a complicated problem.

Another commonly used rhetorical figure is known as *personification,* the assigning of human characteristics to impersonal, nonhuman things. This is often used to create a positive or negative association with something by imbuing it with characteristics the audience may more easily understand. Regular product advertising and marketing campaigns often resort to this. For example, an ad at a service station selling gasoline with additives supposedly able to clean engine parts proclaimed: "Your car's parts are *happier* when they're *cleaner*" (emphasis added to show personification). Of course, engine parts do not feel emotions any more than they have awareness of being dirty or clean—but wording it this way suggests that car parts have feelings like people, rhetorically suggesting that as consumers we should respect their wishes and spring for the more expensive gasoline! Likewise, politicians often employ personification in their speech making. For example, former President Jimmy Carter, in addressing the nation in his 1980 State of the Union speech, employed personification as he described the conflict with the hostage situation in Iran: "In response to the abhorrent situation in Iran, our nation has never been so *aroused* and unified greatly in peacetime. Our position is clear. The United States will not *yield* to blackmail" (emphasis again added to illustrate personification).[20] Can a "nation" be "aroused"? Can it "yield"? Or are these things that people do? How might it have changed Carter's speech if he substituted the word *people* for *nation*?

A final rhetorical figure we might consider is called *prolepsis*, which refers to anticipatory refutation. In this situation, the speaker/rhetor anticipates a criticism or counterargument to the one he or she presents and actually voices the response to it before the opposition can respond. If you have ever watched a student debate in classroom or perhaps a debate between politicians in an election, you will have observed this in practice as one debater argues something to the effect of "In his next speech, my opponent will likely suggest this is not true. But let me tell you why he will be wrong." In this case, the entire reference here is prolepsis because the debater anticipates the criticism and immediately counters it. This is often done to get the response out ahead of the counterargument and perhaps to discourage the opposition from even suggesting it.

Politicians will often use this in their speech making as well. For example, former President Reagan, 2 years into his first administration,[21] once explained his budgeting priorities and answered criticism (before it had been made in response to his speech!) that he was unwilling to help the poor and less fortunate in American society. An exasperated Reagan observed:

> In the discussion of Federal spending, the time has come to put the *sob-sister attempts to portray our desire to get government spending under control as a hard hearted attack on the people of America.* In the first place, even with the economies that we've proposed, spending for entitlements—benefits paid directly to individuals—will actually

increase by one third over the next five years. . . . *Only here in this city of Oz would a budget this big and generous be characterized as a miserly attack on the poor. Now where do some of these attacks originate? They're coming from the very people whose past policies, all done in the name of compassion, brought us the current recession* (emphasis added to show prolepsis).

Reagan was perfectly aware that his discussion of government spending would be criticized by Democrats in the Congress, and, anticipating their arguments, he addressed them directly, voicing the criticism and then supplying the response. Using prolepsis will not completely eliminate the opposition or criticism a speaker/rhetor faces, but it can be a very effective way of dulling the impact of such arguments in advance of their use.

## Public Speaking, Oratory, and Rhetorical Fallacies

On occasion, the president (like many other speakers/rhetors) may want to create the appearance of being rational and reasonable in his rhetoric but will employ tactics that are really anything but logical. When this occurs, rhetorical fallacies are in play. How do they work?

Fallacies are argumentative tactics that operate outside the presence of logic or reasoning. Sometimes explained as logical inconsistencies, these tactics will often be undetectable unless the audience member knows what to look for and demands more logic from the rhetoric. Again, if you have had a class in critical thinking, you will have been exposed to this before. You may be aware that there are literally hundreds of different types of fallacies used by speakers. It is not my intention to restate them all here. Rather, I will address a small list of the more common ones in use by political leaders like the president so that we may add them to our grouping of tools for deconstructing what a president says about terrorism. These fallacies are example reasoning, scare tactics, post hoc ergo propter hoc arguments, reductio ad absurdum claims, and ad hominem attacks.

The fallacy of *example reasoning* is the absence of deductive reasoning. Here, a speaker/rhetor purports to be logical in evidencing his or her conclusion by using evidence from some form of example. This becomes fallacious (and thus, illogical), however, if it is clear that a single example or a limited set of examples has been used, rendering the approach inductive. For example, if the president says that the evidence for a new solution to resolve homelessness can be found in the example of an approach taken by a single city in America, but it turns out that this city has a unique population, not typical of the rest of the country, and the approach has been in operation for only a month, we might say that this argument was a fallacy because of example reasoning. Quite simply, the example would not support the conclusion the president advocated.

Another kind of fallacy commonly used by our leaders is the *scare tactic*. Here, the speaker/rhetor typically overstates or exaggerates a claim for the purpose of trying to scare the audience into submission to his or her message. When your parents swore that they personally knew of someone who had lost an arm that had been waved out of a car window in traffic, they were using this kind of fallacy. It is highly unlikely that they knew of any such individual; their purpose was to scare you into believing that you should keep your hands in the car when they were driving! A president will often resort to the scare tactic fallacy when trying to urgently make a case for something (such as congressional support and funding for a military initiative) by suggesting dire consequences if he does not get what he wants. This is commonly detected when the language and word choice used by the president suggest exaggeration, with the effect of scaring the audience. President Clinton, who made a habit of having his way with the Republican-controlled Congress, often employed this fallacy in successive State of the Union addresses, as well as in Rose Garden press conferences, when arguing against Republican plans to cut his initiatives to "invest in the American future" by paying down the deficit. Clinton would often paint a future doomsday scenario in which generations of Americans would suffer horribly.

The fallacy of *post hoc ergo propter hoc,* while being a mouthful to say out loud, is not as complicated as the name implies. Translated, it means "after the fact, therefore because of the fact." This is a fallacy dealing with the appearance of logical causation. Here, the speaker/rhetor argues that because one result occurred in time *after* the presence of another factor, that the factor must have caused the result. For example, you may recall that in any television murder mystery—such as *Matlock*—an innocent man (soon to be Matlock's client) would often be the "last person to have seen the deceased alive." As such, it was often assumed (fallaciously, of course) that because the murder occurred after the defendant had seen the victim, the defendant must have committed the murder! Programs like this revolved around being able to show that this kind of causal argument would not stand up to reason.

Presidents sometimes use post hoc reasoning in their rhetoric, especially when in the midst of trying to assign blame for something. For example, President Reagan, in his first inaugural address, argued that the economic harm facing the nation as he took office (which included rampant inflation and high unemployment) was the direct result of too much reliance upon the government for solutions. In Reagan's words, "In the present crisis, government is not the solution to our problem; government is the problem." The president's argument, a centerpiece of his populist conservatism in the election, was that the failing economy he inherited in 1980 came about after Jimmy Carter's expanded role for the federal government from 1976 (especially with respect to taxation, and regulation of energy importation and consumption)—and that because the problems came after the federal buildup, they must have been caused by the buildup. The president's argument, however, presented a classic post hoc fallacy. The economic problems facing the country in 1980 were the result of myriad problems; some of them may have been traced to inadequate government policies, but they also included normal cycles of contraction in the economy; decades of poor— or nonexistent—planning at the federal, state, and local level for conservation; no investment in alternate energy forms; and a flailing foreign relations agenda that stretched back through numerous administrations.

The fallacy of *reductio ad absurdum* can be seen in arguments in which a claim is extended through to an extreme position, quite literally *reduced to the absurd*. These kinds of claims are common— especially in marketing and advertising rhetoric. How often are we told, for example, that failure to use certain products may lead to dire and/or embarrassing consequences? One television spot for a product to control the effects of diarrhea argues for its effectiveness but then suggests that failure to use it may subject an individual suffering from diarrhea to the worst of consequences. In the advertising spot, a father who failed to use this particular product is being buried in the sand during a day at the beach when becoming afflicted. At the last instant, in a moment that is funny but patently absurd, he is suddenly struck with the diarrhea but unable to move because he is buried to his neck!

Presidents and other political leaders will, on occasion, rely upon this kind of fallacy in their rhetoric as well. In a famous address critical of television news media, former Vice President Spiro Agnew once complained that there was too much liberal bias in television news (not always true, even when Agnew was in office); that television news exerted too much influence (somewhat accurate—television news was and is extremely influential, as we shall explore in the next chapter); and that decisions about what to show in the news were always based on telling a story that showcased "controversy" (again, a fair claim for television news, even today) but then further opined that the only reason there were so many demonstrations in the streets in protest against the country's involvement in Vietnam was that television news cameras were present. Agnew asked: "How many marches and demonstrations would we have if the marchers did not know that the ever faithful TV cameras would be there to record their antics for the next news shows?" Agnew's conclusion presented a typical reductio fallacy. He began by making reasonable claims (at least in part) but gradually spun the argument until it reached a more absurd conclusion— that the only reason for people to demonstrate en masse against the war in Vietnam was that they thought they might get on television. His claim, of course, ignored the possibility that large public demonstrations against the war might occur because a sizable number of Americans were having serious doubts about what the United States was doing or accomplishing in Southeast Asia.

The fallacy of *ad hominem attacks* occurs when a speaker/ rhetor resorts to name calling in order to advance a claim. We call this approach fallacious because the speaker is suggesting that a course of action should be followed or avoided, not for any rational reason, but simply because an individual or institution associated with the message is a "nasty you-know-what." In many ways, this is more common in the heat of campaigns, when the mudslinging between political camps has increased and the number of days left before the election is limited. The temptation to engage in this fallacy is overwhelming.

Even though it is more typically found in campaigns, this fallacy is often also employed by presidents during their administrations. For example, President Reagan, in a speech now famously remembered for increasing the stakes in the Cold War, once referred to the Soviet Union as the "evil empire." In a similar fashion, the senior President Bush once referred to the government in Iraq as "Nazi." Both claims were fallacious arguments, designed to create public support for U.S. foreign policy against the USSR and Iraq. Reagan's argument was fallacious because calling a country an "evil empire," without explaining what constituted evil, amounted to simplistic name-calling. Likewise, Saddam Hussein's regime may have been repressive (and most likely still is today) and was most assuredly a dangerous dictatorship, but to claim that it was the same as a fascist regime promoting racial purity and world domination was a real stretch. Bush chose the word because Nazism was and is unpopular, and he wanted to make that association in the minds of Americans in order to ensure public support for the Gulf War.

### ❖ CASE STUDIES

Now that we have considered different tools for rhetorically deconstructing a public address or oratory, let us apply these same tools to public speaking by government officials concerning terrorism and begin to assess how these speeches have contributed to our public discourse about the subject and assisted in constructing the meaning of terror. In this chapter, I will use two speeches by President George W. Bush, both made in the month following the attacks of September 11, 2001. In both speeches, paragraphs are numbered, with the number boldfaced and in parentheses at the beginning of each paragraph; this is done so that when I reference the passage in the analysis following each speech, I can identify it for you by the paragraph number. After each speech, I provide full commentary, including audience analysis, description of rhetorical appeals, use of rhetorical figures, and identification of any fallacies. Let us consider each of these in turn.

### President Bush's Speech to the Nation
### Immediately After the Attacks of 9/11

In this first speech, President Bush addresses the nation on the evening of 9/11:

**(1)** Good evening. Today, our fellow citizens, our way of life, our very freedom came under attack in a series of deliberate and deadly terrorist acts. The victims were in airplanes, or in their offices; secretaries, businessmen and women, military and federal workers; moms and dads, friends and neighbors. Thousands of lives were suddenly ended by evil, despicable acts of terror.

**(2)** The pictures of airplanes flying into buildings, fires burning, huge structures collapsing, have filled us with disbelief, terrible sadness, and a quiet, unyielding anger. These acts of mass murder were intended to frighten our nation into chaos and retreat. But they have failed; our country is strong.

**(3)** A great people has been moved to defend a great nation. Terrorist attacks can shake the foundations of our biggest buildings, but they cannot touch the foundation of America. These acts shattered steel, but they cannot dent the steel of American resolve.

**(4)** America was targeted for attack because we're the brightest beacon for freedom and opportunity in the world. And no one will keep that light from shining.

**(5)** Today, our nation saw evil, the very worst of human nature. And we responded with the best of America—with the daring of our rescue workers, with the caring for strangers and neighbors who came to give blood and help in any way they could.

**(6)** Immediately following the first attack, I implemented our government's emergency response plans. Our military is powerful, and it's prepared. Our emergency teams are working in New York City and Washington, D.C. to help with local rescue efforts.

**(7)** Our first priority is to get help to those who have been injured, and to take every precaution to protect our citizens at home and around the world from further attacks.

**(8)** The functions of our government continue without interruption. Federal agencies in Washington which had to be evacuated today are reopening for essential personnel tonight, and will be open for business tomorrow. Our financial institutions remain strong, and the American economy will be open for business, as well.

**(9)** The search is underway for those who are behind these evil acts. I've directed the full resources of our intelligence and law enforcement communities to find those responsible and to bring them to justice. We will make no distinction between the terrorists who committed these acts and those who harbor them.

**(10)**  I appreciate so very much the members of Congress who have joined me in strongly condemning these attacks. And on behalf of the American people, I thank the many world leaders who have called to offer their condolences and assistance.

**(11)**  America and our friends and allies join with all those who want peace and security in the world, and we stand together to win the war against terrorism. Tonight, I ask for your prayers for all those who grieve, for the children whose worlds have been shattered, for all whose sense of safety and security has been threatened. And I pray they will be comforted by a power greater than any of us, spoken through the ages in Psalm 23: "Even though I walk through the valley of the shadow of death, I fear no evil, for You are with me."

**(12)**  This is a day when all Americans from every walk of life unite in our resolve for justice and peace. America has stood down enemies before, and we will do so this time. None of us will ever forget this day. Yet, we go forward to defend freedom and all that is good and just in our world.

**(13)**  Thank you. Good night, and God bless America.

## Audience Analysis of President Bush's September 11 Speech

Here President Bush spoke several hours after the attacks on New York and Washington, D.C., and the crash in Pennsylvania. He was aware that he had not been seen or heard from for much of the time immediately following the attacks and that speculation about his whereabouts (and those of Vice President Dick Cheney) had caused additional anxiety about what was happening.

What can be said about the audience or audiences for his speech? First, we know that even though the speech was broadcast in the evening, the president and his speechwriters could absolutely assume they had the attention of almost anyone within sight of a television set or computer monitor or within earshot of a radio. Unlike most presidential addresses (even popular ones like a State of the Union or the

Inaugural Address), this was a relatively short speech that would command widespread attention. The president speaks to multiple audiences in this address.

First and foremost, he addresses all Americans—including both political allies and opponents. After a day's worth of extensive media coverage of the attacks (and most especially, the video footage of the jets flying into the WTC), he could be sure that everyone in the domestic audience had already seen the attacks, or knew of them, and would be concerned. As mentioned earlier in this chapter, in times of political crisis with international repercussions, the president generally speaks with a single voice for the country at large. On this night, he could also safely assume that no one—including his opponents in the Democratic party who might still have been questioning his legitimacy after the Florida election results—would challenge his leadership or what he had to say about the attacks on our country. Though he acknowledges members of the Congress in Paragraph 10, he does not address political insiders as allies or opponents in this speech. Instead, he simply assumes that they are all part of the larger domestic audience of Americans, as shaken and concerned as anyone else. Within that context, his message (as we shall see when we assess his use of appeals) could be general for all Americans. Using the terminology addressed before, we could categorize this initial audience as sympathetic—even if it contained traditional opponents.

A second audience for this speech includes the larger international community of nations, although here Bush is more careful to divide his comments between America's friends and opponents. Friends and allies of America are defined in this speech in Paragraph 11 as those who want peace and security in the world. Although Bush does not identify any allied nations by name, he assumes that most people in the audience will already have been exposed to news reports of international condemnation for the attacks by other countries across the globe. Like the domestic audience, we might consider this audience to be sympathetic to the speech message.

By contrast, in Paragraph 9 he labels our opponents as either those who have directly participated in this terrorism or those countries who, by giving sanctuary to terrorists, have allowed the attacks to occur. Again, here he does not name names because at this point in the day, there is still no hard and clear evidence about exactly who is responsible for what (at least, if there is such evidence, Bush isn't sharing it in this speech). Nevertheless, the president addresses this audience of opponents who might have given sanctuary or support to terrorists, emphasizing the beginnings of a new policy for the United States: that in hunting down those responsible for the attacks, the United States will not distinguish between sponsors, nation-hosts, sanctuary givers, or the actual terrorists themselves.

Finally, the president's speech also addresses those directly responsible for the terror of that day. Although he does not (and perhaps cannot at this point) identify them specifically, he simply refers to them and their actions as "evil" in Paragraphs 1 and 9.

### Selection of Rhetorical Appeals

Given that the first and perhaps most important audience Bush addresses is the American public, he quickly fashions a message that addresses their (our) immediate concerns of the day. In Paragraphs 1 to 4, Bush acknowledges the prior exposure via mass media of this audience to the attacks of the day, but he quickly argues that although the country has been shaken by the terror, it has not been fundamentally diminished or weakened. Bush's description of the attacks is vivid and graphic—though no different from what people have already been exposed to on television. These specific references are largely pathos oriented, designed to remind the country of the mood it is feeling, which, in the words of the president in Paragraph 2, hovers between "disbelief, terrible sadness, and a quiet, unyielding anger."

In Paragraph 4, the president feigns an attempt at a logos-centered claim when he attempts an explanation for why the United States was attacked. Here, he suggests that we were targeted because "we're the brightest beacon for freedom and opportunity in the world." If this were reconstituted as a syllogism with premises and a conclusion, it would look like the following:

*Major Premise:* Terrorists target and attack those who promote freedom and opportunity.

*Minor Premise:* America is the brightest beacon for freedom and opportunity.

*Conclusion:* Terrorists targeted America because we (America) are the brightest beacon for freedom and opportunity.

Does this use of logos make sense to you? Both premises must be accurate and defensible in order for the conclusion to follow and the syllogism to be effective; are both premises defensible here? Taking them in reverse order for the moment, the second premise (the minor premise) may be defensible, depending upon how one defines "freedom and opportunity." Ours is a relatively free society and generally open and accessible to all who make it here legally.

What about the major premise? Is it true that terrorists attack those who promote freedom and opportunity? Here, the logic is less compelling. Bush never explains why terrorists would oppose either freedom or opportunity. He never gives other examples or offers any evidence for this claim—and as such, it comes off sounding flat. But that may not really matter for the initial audience of Americans. The president's use of pathos in the first few paragraphs has identified for us how we are feeling; intellectualizing the reasons for a terror attack can come later.

Bush's other primary appeal for this initial audience involves a greater blend of ethos. Remember that many were wondering who was in charge immediately after the attacks. Of course, today we know that the Secret Service was merely following protocol in sequestering the president in the face of the attack and making sure he was kept separate from the vice president (so that both would not be targeted for assassination at the same time, creating a void at the top of the executive branch). But on that night, the president needed to reassure people that he was in charge and in control of the situation. In a sense, he needed to use language to communicate his ethos as leader and authority figure. He does this in Paragraphs 6 to 9 as he describes the initiatives he has set into motion in responding to the crisis.

For America's allies—who look to the United States as the dominant superpower in the world—Bush offers thanks for the condolences and assistance in Paragraphs 11 to 12, and he tries to reassure them that this country has not been permanently damaged economically in Paragraph 9, suggesting that the economy remains strong and "will be open for business." These are mostly ethos appeals, as Bush tries to impart the personal strength he suggests for himself to the country as a whole.

For America's enemies, the president's use of the above is intended to suggest that the attacks have not achieved their objectives (shutting us down, paralyzing us), and in Paragraph 9, the president offers a blend of ethos (speaking as the commander-in-chief) and pathos when he suggests that those responsible will be brought to justice and punished.

### Figures and Fallacies in the September 11 Speech

This speech is short and fairly to the point. The single attempt at logos is, as indicated before, at worst weak and at best underevidenced or explained. In that way, Bush's use of logic is to some degree fallacious—but we must remember that in this speech, the audience analysis was not necessarily dictating a lengthy, logical message. Americans needed to be reassured that they had a strong leader who empathized with their suffering and anger. Our allies needed to know that we appreciated their concern and that we were still the same superpower they had depended on 24 hours earlier. Our enemies needed to know that the United States would not let this attack go unpunished. In that rhetorical situation, logic and reasoning were beside the point.

The president does, however, make use of some figures to get his message across to the multiple audiences. In Paragraphs 6 to 9, he uses catalogue to list all the actions he has taken to respond to the attacks as a way of communicating his ethos as a leader.

In Paragraph 5, he employs antithesis when he sets clauses in opposition to each other. Here, he casts "evil" and "the very worst of human nature" in opposition to the "best of America" to illustrate the moral correctness of our position as victims of terror and again to communicate to the terrorists that ultimately they have failed in their attempts.

In Paragraph 12, President Bush also employs personification, assigning human, personal characteristics to a nonhuman, nonpersonal thing, when he suggests that "America has *stood down* enemies before." Used in this way, America is compared to a single, strong individual, unafraid to stand up to bullies and villains. This is meant to boost confidence in the American audience, while again suggesting to the terrorists what fates await them in the future.

### Bush's Speech to the Congress, the Nation, and the World, September 20, 2001

The second speech we will examine from President Bush is an address dated September 20, 2001:

**(1)**    Mr. Speaker, Mr. President Pro Tempore, members of Congress, and fellow Americans:

**(2)**    In the normal course of events, Presidents come to this chamber to report on the state of the Union. Tonight, no such report is needed. It has already been delivered by the American people.

**(3)**    We have seen it in the courage of passengers, who rushed terrorists to save others on the ground—passengers like an exceptional man named Todd Beamer. And would you please help me to welcome his wife, Lisa Beamer, here tonight. (Applause.)

**(4)**    We have seen the state of our Union in the endurance of rescuers, working past exhaustion. We have seen the unfurling of flags, the lighting of candles, the giving of blood, the saying of prayers—in English, Hebrew, and Arabic. We have seen the decency of a loving and giving people who have made the grief of strangers their own.

**(5)**    My fellow citizens, for the last nine days, the entire world has seen for itself the state of our Union—and it is strong. (Applause.)

**(6)**    Tonight we are a country awakened to danger and called to defend freedom. Our grief has turned to anger, and anger to resolution. Whether we bring our enemies to justice, or bring justice to our enemies, justice will be done. (Applause.)

**(7)**    I thank the Congress for its leadership at such an important time. All of America was touched on the evening of the tragedy to see Republicans and Democrats joined together on the steps of this Capitol, singing "God Bless America." And you did more than sing; you acted, by delivering $40 billion to rebuild our communities and meet the needs of our military.

**(8)**    Speaker Hastert, Minority Leader Gephardt, Majority Leader Daschle and Senator Lott, I thank you for your friendship, for your leadership and for your service to our country. (Applause.)

**(9)**    And on behalf of the American people, I thank the world for its outpouring of support. America will never forget the sounds of our National Anthem playing at Buckingham Palace, on the streets of Paris, and at Berlin's Brandenburg Gate.

**(10)**    We will not forget South Korean children gathering to pray outside our embassy in Seoul, or the prayers of sympathy offered at a mosque in Cairo. We will not forget moments of silence and days of mourning in Australia and Africa and Latin America.

**(11)**    Nor will we forget the citizens of 80 other nations who died with our own: dozens of Pakistanis; more than 130 Israelis; more than 250 citizens of India; men and women from El Salvador, Iran, Mexico and Japan; and hundreds of British citizens. America has no truer friend than Great Britain. (Applause.) Once again, we are joined together in a great cause—so honored the British Prime Minister has crossed an ocean to show his unity of purpose with America. Thank you for coming, friend. (Applause.)

**(12)**    On September the 11th, enemies of freedom committed an act of war against our country. Americans have known wars—but for the past 136 years, they have been wars on foreign soil, except for one Sunday in 1941. Americans have known the casualties of war—but not at the center of a great city on a peaceful morning. Americans have known surprise attacks—but never before on thousands of civilians. All of this was brought upon us in a single day—and night fell on a different world, a world where freedom itself is under attack. Americans have many questions tonight. Americans are asking: Who attacked our country? The evidence we have gathered all points to a collection of loosely affiliated terrorist organizations known as al Qaeda. They are the same murderers indicted for bombing American embassies in Tanzania and Kenya, and responsible for bombing the USS Cole.

**(13)**  al Qaeda is to terror what the Mafia is to crime. But its goal is not making money; its goal is remaking the world—and imposing its radical beliefs on people everywhere.

**(14)**  The terrorists practice a fringe form of Islamic extremism that has been rejected by Muslim scholars and the vast majority of Muslim clerics—a fringe movement that perverts the peaceful teachings of Islam. The terrorists' directive commands them to kill Christians and Jews, to kill all Americans, and make no distinction among military and civilians, including women and children.

**(15)**  This group and its leader—a person named Osama bin Laden—are linked to many other organizations in different countries, including the Egyptian Islamic Jihad and the Islamic Movement of Uzbekistan. There are thousands of these terrorists in more than 60 countries. They are recruited from their own nations and neighborhoods and brought to camps in places like Afghanistan, where they are trained in the tactics of terror. They are sent back to their homes or sent to hide in countries around the world to plot evil and destruction.

**(16)**  The leadership of al Qaeda has great influence in Afghanistan and supports the Taliban regime in controlling most of that country. In Afghanistan, we see al Qaeda's vision for the world.

**(17)**  Afghanistan's people have been brutalized—many are starving and many have fled. Women are not allowed to attend school. You can be jailed for owning a television. Religion can be practiced only as their leaders dictate. A man can be jailed in Afghanistan if his beard is not long enough.

**(18)**  The United States respects the people of Afghanistan— after all, we are currently its largest source of humanitarian aid—but we condemn the Taliban regime. (Applause.) It is not only repressing its own people, it is threatening people everywhere by sponsoring and sheltering and supplying terrorists. By aiding and abetting murder, the Taliban regime is committing murder.

**(19)**   And tonight, the United States of America makes the following demands on the Taliban: Deliver to United States authorities all the leaders of al Qaeda who hide in your land. (Applause.) Release all foreign nationals, including American citizens, you have unjustly imprisoned. Protect foreign journalists, diplomats and aid workers in your country. Close immediately and permanently every terrorist training camp in Afghanistan, and hand over every terrorist, and every person in their support structure, to appropriate authorities. (Applause.) Give the United States full access to terrorist training camps, so we can make sure they are no longer operating.

**(20)**   These demands are not open to negotiation or discussion. (Applause.) The Taliban must act, and act immediately. They will hand over the terrorists, or they will share in their fate.

**(21)**   I also want to speak tonight directly to Muslims throughout the world. We respect your faith. It's practiced freely by many millions of Americans, and by millions more in countries that America counts as friends. Its teachings are good and peaceful, and those who commit evil in the name of Allah blaspheme the name of Allah. (Applause.) The terrorists are traitors to their own faith, trying, in effect, to hijack Islam itself. The enemy of America is not our many Muslim friends; it is not our many Arab friends. Our enemy is a radical network of terrorists, and every government that supports them. (Applause.)

**(22)**   Our war on terror begins with al Qaeda, but it does not end there. It will not end until every terrorist group of global reach has been found, stopped and defeated. (Applause.)

**(23)**   Americans are asking, why do they hate us? They hate what we see right here in this chamber—a democratically elected government. Their leaders are self-appointed. They hate our freedoms—our freedom of religion, our freedom of speech, our freedom to vote and assemble and disagree with each other.

**(24)** They want to overthrow existing governments in many Muslim countries, such as Egypt, Saudi Arabia, and Jordan. They want to drive Israel out of the Middle East. They want to drive Christians and Jews out of vast regions of Asia and Africa.

**(25)** These terrorists kill not merely to end lives, but to disrupt and end a way of life. With every atrocity, they hope that America grows fearful, retreating from the world and forsaking our friends. They stand against us, because we stand in their way.

**(26)** We are not deceived by their pretenses to piety. We have seen their kind before. They are the heirs of all the murderous ideologies of the 20th century. By sacrificing human life to serve their radical visions—by abandoning every value except the will to power—they follow in the path of fascism, and Nazism, and totalitarianism. And they will follow that path all the way, to where it ends: in history's unmarked grave of discarded lies. (Applause.)

**(27)** Americans are asking: How will we fight and win this war? We will direct every resource at our command—every means of diplomacy, every tool of intelligence, every instrument of law enforcement, every financial influence, and every necessary weapon of war—to the disruption and to the defeat of the global terror network.

**(28)** This war will not be like the war against Iraq a decade ago, with a decisive liberation of territory and a swift conclusion. It will not look like the air war above Kosovo two years ago, where no ground troops were used and not a single American was lost in combat.

**(29)** Our response involves far more than instant retaliation and isolated strikes. Americans should not expect one battle, but a lengthy campaign, unlike any other we have ever seen. It may include dramatic strikes, visible on TV, and covert operations, secret even in success. We will starve terrorists of funding, turn them one against another, drive them from place to place, until there is no refuge or no rest. And we will pursue nations that provide aid or safe haven to terrorism. Every nation, in every region, now has a decision to make. Either you are with us, or you are with the terrorists. (Applause.) From this day forward, any nation that continues to harbor or support terrorism will be regarded by the United States as a hostile regime.

(30) Our nation has been put on notice: We are not immune from attack. We will take defensive measures against terrorism to protect Americans. Today, dozens of federal departments and agencies, as well as state and local governments, have responsibilities affecting homeland security. These efforts must be coordinated at the highest level. So tonight I announce the creation of a Cabinet-level position reporting directly to me—the Office of Homeland Security.

(31) And tonight I also announce a distinguished American to lead this effort, to strengthen American security: a military veteran, an effective governor, a true patriot, a trusted friend—Pennsylvania's Tom Ridge. (Applause.) He will lead, oversee and coordinate a comprehensive national strategy to safeguard our country against terrorism, and respond to any attacks that may come.

(32) These measures are essential. But the only way to defeat terrorism as a threat to our way of life is to stop it, eliminate it, and destroy it where it grows. (Applause.)

(33) Many will be involved in this effort, from FBI agents to intelligence operatives to the reservists we have called to active duty. All deserve our thanks, and all have our prayers. And tonight, a few miles from the damaged Pentagon, I have a message for our military: Be ready. I've called the Armed Forces to alert, and there is a reason. The

hour is coming when America will act, and you will make us proud. (Applause.)

**(34)** This is not, however, just America's fight. And what is at stake is not just America's freedom. This is the world's fight. This is civilization's fight. This is the fight of all who believe in progress and pluralism, tolerance and freedom.

**(35)** We ask every nation to join us. We will ask, and we will need, the help of police forces, intelligence services, and banking systems around the world. The United States is grateful that many nations and many international organizations have already responded—with sympathy and with support. Nations from Latin America, to Asia, to Africa, to Europe, to the Islamic world. Perhaps the NATO Charter reflects best the attitude of the world: An attack on one is an attack on all.

**(36)** The civilized world is rallying to America's side. They understand that if this terror goes unpunished, their own cities, their own citizens may be next. Terror, unanswered, can not only bring down buildings, it can threaten the stability of legitimate governments. And you know what— we're not going to allow it. (Applause.)

**(37)** Americans are asking: What is expected of us? I ask you to live your lives, and hug your children. I know many citizens have fears tonight, and I ask you to be calm and resolute, even in the face of a continuing threat.

**(38)** I ask you to uphold the values of America, and remember why so many have come here. We are in a fight for our principles, and our first responsibility is to live by them. No one should be singled out for unfair treatment or unkind words because of their ethnic background or religious faith. (Applause.)

**(39)** I ask you to continue to support the victims of this tragedy with your contributions. Those who want to give can go to a central source of information, libertyunites.org, to find the names of groups providing direct help in New York, Pennsylvania, and Virginia.

**(40)** The thousands of FBI agents who are now at work in this investigation may need your cooperation, and I ask you to give it.

**(41)** I ask for your patience, with the delays and inconveniences that may accompany tighter security; and for your patience in what will be a long struggle.

**(42)** I ask your continued participation and confidence in the American economy. Terrorists attacked a symbol of American prosperity. They did not touch its source. America is successful because of the hard work, and creativity, and enterprise of our people. These were the true strengths of our economy before September 11th, and they are our strengths today. (Applause.)

**(43)** And, finally, please continue praying for the victims of terror and their families, for those in uniform, and for our great country. Prayer has comforted us in sorrow, and will help strengthen us for the journey ahead.

**(44)** Tonight I thank my fellow Americans for what you have already done and for what you will do. And ladies and gentlemen of the Congress, I thank you, their representatives, for what you have already done and for what we will do together.

**(45)** Tonight, we face new and sudden national challenges. We will come together to improve air safety, to dramatically expand the number of air marshals on domestic flights, and take new measures to prevent hijacking. We will come together to promote stability and keep our airlines flying, with direct assistance during this emergency. (Applause.)

**(46)** We will come together to give law enforcement the additional tools it needs to track down terror here at home. (Applause.) We will come together to strengthen our intelligence capabilities to know the plans of terrorists before they act, and find them before they strike. (Applause.)

**(47)** We will come together to take active steps that strengthen America's economy, and put our people back to work.

**(48)** Tonight we welcome two leaders who embody the extraordinary spirit of all New Yorkers: Governor George Pataki, and Mayor Rudolph Giuliani. (Applause.) As a symbol of America's resolve, my administration will work with Congress, and these two leaders, to show the world that we will rebuild New York City. (Applause.)

**(49)** After all that has just passed—all the lives taken, and all the possibilities and hopes that died with them—it is natural to wonder if America's future is one of fear. Some speak of an age of terror. I know there are struggles ahead, and dangers to face. But this country will define our times, not be defined by them. As long as the United States of America is determined and strong, this will not be an age of terror; this will be an age of liberty, here and across the world. (Applause.)

**(50)** Great harm has been done to us. We have suffered great loss. And in our grief and anger we have found our mission and our moment. Freedom and fear are at war. The advance of human freedom—the great achievement of our time, and the great hope of every time—now depends on us. Our nation—this generation—will lift a dark threat of violence from our people and our future. We will rally the world to this cause by our efforts, by our courage. We will not tire, we will not falter, and we will not fail. (Applause.)

**(51)** It is my hope that in the months and years ahead, life will return almost to normal. We'll go back to our lives and routines, and that is good. Even grief recedes with time and grace. But our resolve must not pass. Each of us will remember what happened that day, and to whom it happened. We'll remember the moment the news came—where we were and what we were doing. Some will remember an image of a fire, or a story of rescue. Some will carry memories of a face and a voice gone forever.

**(52)** And I will carry this: It is the police shield of a man named George Howard, who died at the World Trade Center trying to save others. It was given to me by his mom, Arlene, as a proud memorial to her son. This is my reminder of lives that ended, and a task that does not end. (Applause.)

**(53)** I will not forget this wound to our country or those who inflicted it. I will not yield; I will not rest; I will not relent in waging this struggle for freedom and security for the American people.

**(54)** The course of this conflict is not known, yet its outcome is certain. Freedom and fear, justice and cruelty, have always been at war, and we know that God is not neutral between them. (Applause.)

**(55)** Fellow citizens, we'll meet violence with patient justice— assured of the rightness of our cause, and confident of the victories to come. In all that lies before us, may God grant us wisdom, and may He watch over the United States of America.

**(56)** Thank you. (Applause.)

### Audience Analysis of the September 20, 2001, Speech

Here, President Bush is addressing many of the same audiences he did in the speech on September 11. Again, there is the appeal to Americans and to our allies, as well as a more pointed message to both the nations sponsoring or hosting terrorists and, of course, the terrorists themselves. These are, respectively, sympathetic audiences (Americans and allied countries of the United States) and hostile audiences (terrorists and nations that sponsor or give refuge to terror). But in this speech, one finds that the president has decided to broaden the range of audiences.

First, in Paragraphs 21 to 26, Bush turns to an audience segment that may cut across sympathetic, neutral, and hostile audience groups, depending upon where these audience members reside, as he addresses Muslims both in the United States and abroad. Mindful that within days after 9/11, some American citizens of Muslim faith were harassed because of false assumptions about their faith and an assumed connection to the attacks, as well as rampant media speculation about which other nations might have been connected to the attacks (most of the speculation centering on nations with large Muslim populations), the president is careful to distinguish the perpetrators of the attacks from Muslims generally. When he says: "The enemy of America is not our many Muslim friends; it is not our many Arab friends. Our enemy is a radical network of terrorists, and every government that supports them," he is attempting to narrow the list of those responsible, making it possible for people to fill the ranks of the neutral or sympathetic audience for his message.

At the same time, there were, by inference, neutral audience members to this speech as well—most likely in those nations who might feel sympathy for victims of the terrorist attacks but who might not otherwise feel inclined to U.S. foreign policy in the Middle East politically or be much inclined to sign on to a military campaign generally. When Bush states in Paragraph 29 that "either you are with us, or you are against us," he is putting these audience members on notice that they can no longer be neutral in this affair; they will have to pick sides, and the consequences for picking the wrong side will be severe.

Notice that while this speech follows Bush's previous address by only 9 days, the amount of detail and the extent to which he is forthcoming are much greater in this second speech. Now, many of the answers he was unwilling or unable to provide in the immediate aftermath of the attacks are made clearer. The motivations for this can be found again in the audiences Bush addresses. Bush is aware that much media attention and general public discourse has been devoted to speculation about who was responsible and why they attacked. In this speech, he does his best to answer those questions for the more general American audience, while also using the answers he gives as a beginning justification for the argument he will make to other nations—allies and enemies—about picking sides. Bush is also much more direct about whom he believes our allies and our enemies to be. Unlike the address of 9/11, this speech identifies countries, terrorist groups, and specific individuals.

**Selection of Rhetorical Appeals**

As before, it is critical that the American audience perceive Bush the messenger as a strong, authoritative leader. Understandably, 9/11 was perhaps too soon after the attack for him to be anything but general in his remarks about the attacks. Although he had announced some initiatives as of 9/11, here he is far more specific about what he wants to do in response to the threat from terrorism. In Paragraphs 30 and 31, he announces the creation of a new cabinet-level position, called the Office of Homeland Security, to be headed by Tom Ridge and charged with the coordination of federal, state, and local efforts involving homeland security.

In Paragraphs 19 to 20, 22, and 27 to 29, he makes the case for demanding immediate concessions from Afghanistan and threatening (or really promising) war on al Qaeda. Both the creation of the new cabinet position and the promise of war are targeted to showcase Bush's ethos with the audience and to reinforce his authority as our leader.

Additionally—and in contrast to his address of 9/11—Bush here resorts to a familiar rhetorical approach to ethos, typical of traditional presidential addresses such as a State of the Union speech. Notice in Paragraphs 3 and 52 how Bush makes reference to the sacrifice of Todd Beamer, one of the individuals killed in the plane crash in Pennsylvania as passengers sought to retake the plane, and later to Officer George Howard, one of the rescuers killed in the World Trade Center. He references these two men by name and then indicates (respectively) Beamer's widow and Howard's mother, who are present at the speech. Bush derives ethos from both men and their respective families. They were heroes and martyrs, and Bush derives strength from their examples. Notice also that he opens his speech this way and closes it in the same way—both of which indicate the degree to which he perceives this kind of derived ethos is significant to the American audience.

Like the address of 9/11, this speech is filled with pathos-oriented rhetoric, targeted not only to the American audience but also to the different countries in the international community. Both the aforementioned examples of Beamer and Howard also serve as pathos in this speech, for they are sad, emotional examples of sacrifice and courage. Additionally, in Paragraph 4, Bush references the symbolic responses of people in America (unfurling flags, lighting candles, giving blood, and praying), and later, in Paragraphs 9 to 11, he describes the international response of support from Europe, parts of Asia, Africa, Australia, and Latin America. Each international episode he cites (prayers of sympathy offered at a mosque in Cairo, the United States' national anthem being played at the Brandenburg Gate in Berlin, even the presence of British Prime Minister Tony Blair in the audience for Bush's speech) are designed to be emotional and showcase support for the position he will advance in his war against terrorism.

Of necessity, Bush does go back to a logos message in this speech as well when he attempts to explain who was responsible for the attacks. In Paragraphs 12 to 16, he identifies al Qaeda as the terrorist organization responsible for the attacks, Osama bin Laden as the leader of al Qaeda, and Afghanistan as the country responsible for hosting al Qaeda. He creates the appearance of logos in these passages by suggesting that "evidence we have gathered points to a collection of loosely affiliated terrorist organizations known as al Qaeda." In Paragraph 18, he focuses on Afghanistan, which will be the initial theater for military operations in the "war on terror," and constructs what appears to be another attempt at deductive logic when he explains that those who aid and abet murder are themselves guilty of murder. This time, his implied syllogism appears to be more defensible. It looks like this:

> *Major Premise:* All those who aid and abet murder are guilty of committing murder.
>
> *Minor Premise:* The Taliban (the authority in Afghanistan at the time) aids and abets murder by giving sanctuary to al Qaeda.
>
> *Conclusion:* By aiding and abetting murder, the Taliban is guilty of committing murder.

As a matter of criminal law and public understanding in this country, the major premise is not a controversial statement. Federal and state criminal laws[22] recognize such a distinction and routinely prosecute those who aid and abet murder. Likewise, the minor premise—suggesting that the Taliban aids and abets al Qaeda by giving it sanctuary—is openly recognized. If these premises are accurate, the conclusion regarding the Taliban and committing murder must follow. At least, that is the way it appears at first blush.

This use of logos is necessary not only for the American audience—whose backing Bush will need in the coming war in Afghanistan—but also for the international community of allies, whose logistical, political, and/or military support he may require in the military campaign that is all but preordained in this speech. Americans have to be satisfied that there is a reason (beyond revenge) to go into a war that may, in the president's words, become an indefinite "lengthy campaign" (Paragraph 29), within which America may well suffer real casualties. Likewise, our international allies need to be assured that there is a semblance of reason and fact (beyond the impulse for a pound of flesh) for a military campaign, lest they be accused of backing America in an imperialist campaign against a smaller, poorer nation. Especially important here are those allies in Arab countries such as Egypt, whose support the United States has in this affair, but whose people may share a different perspective, fearing American retaliation against Afghanistan as a plot against Islam, another perceived effort at imperialism, or yet another case of what they see as an American foreign policy that favors Israel over other Middle Eastern countries. For leaders in countries such as Egypt to be able to sell their support of the U.S. position, logos informed by facts and evidence may be a better tool than ethos or pathos.

### Rhetorical Figures and Fallacies

Stylistically, the president employs a series of rhetorical questions throughout the speech to advance the general structure of his address. At Paragraphs 12, 23, 27, and 37, he voices questions that he assumes his American audience would like to ask. In a way, this approach is a form of prolepsis in that here he anticipates the questions (which have already been voiced as criticisms from Americans who do not understand why the attacks occurred or what the administration is planning to do about them). Bush voices the questions and then supplies the answers in a way that not only speaks to the American audience but creates a framework for the messages to the other audiences as well. For example, when in Paragraph 12 he says, "Americans are asking: Who attacked our country?" he then supplies the answer—identifying al Qaeda—as a means to suggest for the larger audience what he will do to terrorists and what he may do to Afghanistan. It is there that Bush reminds all other nations that they must pick sides in this fight.

Bush makes use of many other figures in this speech as well. First among these is the use of anaphora in Paragraphs 3 and 4, where he suggests, "We have seen it," and in Paragraph 50, where he notes that "*we will* rally the world to this cause by our efforts, by our courage. *We will* not tire, *we will* not falter, and *we will* not fail." By continually beginning each portion with "we will," he makes our response a collective response, for both the United States and the international community.

Another figure featuring prominently in this speech is antithesis, which Bush uses in Paragraphs 6 ("Whether we *bring our enemies to justice,* or *bring justice to our enemies*"), 49 ("But our *country will define our times, not be defined by them*"), and 50 ("*Freedom* and *fear* are at war"), each time to show sharp contrast between the United States' options for dealing with terrorism. When he describes the first of these in Paragraph 6, the contrast is meant to indicate that we may go through traditional legal channels to arrest and prosecute those responsible or that we may use our military superiority to attack and eliminate the threat in a way that (as the euphemism suggests) "brings justice." Likewise, when he suggests in Paragraph 49 that our country will define our times rather than be defined by them, he is really arguing that our government will not be passive and reactive but rather active and assumptive in dealing with terror. The final use of antithesis, in Paragraph 50, is meant to reduce and simplify our conflict with terror to a simple choice between "freedom" (for the United States and her allies) and "fear" (practiced and spread by terrorists as a means of achieving their goals). The antithesis here is perhaps overly simplistic, but Bush intends to inspire his sympathetic American and allied country audiences and to warn those neutral audience members that their choice is not just between the United States and terrorists but implicitly between freedom and fear.

The president employs accumulation in Paragraph 27 when he uses several examples—all of which are basically diplomatic and military tools at the disposal of the United States—that he asserts will disrupt and defeat global terror

Catalogue is employed by Bush in Paragraphs 2 to 4 to list all the ways Americans have demonstrated courage, sacrifice, and patriotism, and later in Paragraphs 9 to 11 as he lists the examples of support from the international community. Here, the emphasis is on volume, trying to give depth to the emotional appeal of the individual examples he cites.

Bush also uses personification in this address: In Paragraph 6, he suggests that the country is "awakened to danger," treating our country as an individual and imbuing us with individual characteristics—such as awakening, or coming to a new sense of awareness. The impact of this is to suggest that we are a collective whole, all thinking the same way on this issue. He makes use of personification again in the closing words to the speech when he reminds us that he will not forget the "wound to our country" (Paragraph 53).

The president also makes extensive use of fallacies in this speech, including ad hominem attacks, example reasoning, post hoc ergo propter hoc, reductio ad absurdum, and scare tactics.

In Paragraph 13, the president compares al Qaeda to the Mafia, a well-known criminal network. The effect is to give the American audience a way to understand "who attacked our country" by instantly labeling the terrorists with a comparison to something they already know and fear. Some may argue the comparison is not fallacious because both terrorists and Mafiosi are prone to violence, but the parallels are not so strong. The Mafia engages in criminal enterprise—including the use of violence—for profit; terrorists, by contrast, have widely different motivations for their use or threats of violence. Comparing the terrorists of al Qaeda to the Mafia, however, allows us to draw on representations of gangsters and organized criminals in popular culture and to see terrorists in the same light.

In Paragraph 35, Bush employs the fallacy of example reasoning when he cites the NATO Charter to demonstrate why all nations have a stake in battling terrorism and says: "An attack on one is an attack on all." This kind of evidence for his claim of international support perhaps makes the most sense for our allies in Western Europe who are currently members of NATO—but he references other continents (e.g., Asia and Africa, as well as the Islamic world—by which, one presumes, he means the Middle East), who are not and will never be members of NATO, as regions whose nations might also believe this. In point of fact, many of these other countries, though perhaps feeling sympathy for the United States in the 9/11 attacks, have their own problems at home with terrorism and seldom act in unified ways to respond to them. Equally important, not even NATO members always agree about responding collectively when the interests of NATO member nations are challenged.[23]

A post hoc fallacy can be seen in the president's attempt at logic as he builds the argument that those who aid and abet murder are actually murderers themselves. In Paragraphs 17 to 19, he begins by suggesting that the Taliban was responsible for giving shelter to al Qaeda and therefore for helping cause the violence this terrorist group practiced. Because the attacks of 9/11 came *after* the Taliban's willingness to host this group, Bush argues that the Taliban must have helped cause the attack (after the fact, therefore because of the fact). Of course, there is no proof offered at this point in the speech (or any speech he had given to that date) that the Taliban actively approved of and sponsored the attacks of 9/11. And Bush seems to be aware he will be accused of fallacious argumentation if he persists in this, for it is at this point that he shifts his argument to the syllogism articulated earlier. Whether or not the Taliban actually participated in the sponsoring of the attack, Bush says, giving any aid to those who commit murder makes the individual who gives the aid equally responsible for the murder.

Finally, the president also employs an example of reductio ad absurdum fallacy in Paragraph 26 when he suggests that terrorists are like those who used ideology to rationalize murder earlier in the past century and then calls these groups by name—fascists, Nazis, totalitarians—and adds that, like them, terrorists will find their ideologies in the graveyard of "discarded lies." At this point, however, the president has provided no evidence or explanation of the motives for these attacks, other than claiming that these terrorists hate freedom and countries like the United States that promote freedom. He has also already added that they cannot claim Islam as the religious, ideological basis for their motivation, so what is the ideology they practice? Why is it like fascism—or Nazism? The further Bush goes with this point, the less it makes sense—although one must admit that it sounds and reads well.

Despite a critical review of the rhetorical approach used by the president, this speech was still very effective in reaching its different audiences—most especially the primary sympathetic audience in America and her allies, as well as the possibly neutral audience of some countries in the international community who were noncommittal about a military incursion into Afghanistan. Although Bush is actually quite lean on specific details and the evidence he claims to have, he does name names and identify nation-sponsors and a terror organization in this speech. The details give those in the sympathetic audience enough to frame the outline of our discourse about 9/11, correcting and smoothing out the rough speculation we may have learned from endless priming in news and popular media. By the conclusion of this speech, the sympathetic audience has the president's official version of the facts: Osama bin Laden and his organization (al Qaeda) were responsible for the attacks, and Afghanistan is the country that played host to them, and therefore the country that must now give them up or face the wrath of the United States and her allies. Of course, this suggests that a physical response from the United States will be forthcoming—and although the president can speak for the nation in foreign affairs, it is evident he wants their (our) blessings before proceeding. To that end, he is careful to still cast the attack *and our response* in moral terms, reducing this to a simple fight between good and evil. In the president's rhetoric, all terrorism and terrorists are evil, whereas the United States (now the victim) represents what is good and decent. Domestically, at least, the president's reduction of terrorism and 9/11 to a fight between good and evil again helps to shape public discourse by implying that the choice for understanding terrorism and what must be done in response is relatively simple. Some may point out that this only reflects the president's style, which is to speak in plain language—but the reduction of this complex problem to something so simple also helps to mute criticism of the administration or its response. When the president says this is about good and evil—and he speaks for us—then we talk about 9/11 in the same way, perhaps with the same simplicity. What critical questions do we ask when the discourse is at this level? Are there questions about prior American foreign policy and the Taliban? Or are there questions about the involvement of our own CIA with the Mujahadeen in their fight against the old Soviet Union? Is there discussion about our foreign policy in the Middle East toward wealthy oil-producing nations like Saudi Arabia—or toward Israel?

It is in this last point that the president begins to find some disagreement in the international community, within which some countries (including some in Europe) do not feel the problem of terrorism is anywhere near as simplistic as he represents. Many feel that the problem he has identified is genuine and acknowledge the right and responsibility of the United States to respond with force, but also suggest that the problem is complicated and may require a more nuanced, sophisticated analysis. By framing the argument about terrorism as the president has done, the complexity in the issue is left to the larger international audience, and, given the media coverage of the issue, not always in a manner that allows for diverse points of view.

For our discourse at home, reducing this equation to a choice between simplistic extremes was also reinforced by making support for the president's position a measure of one's patriotism. Indeed, one strong effect of both terror violence and destruction on 9/11, *as well as* the president's statements about the same, has been to encourage many in the American audience to reconsider what patriotism and love of this country means. Part of the American public discourse about the terrorism of 9/11 was to rediscover a sense of patriotism, often expressed in the symbol of the American flag. In the weeks and months following the attacks of 9/11 and the president's own rhetoric about the subject, large national chain stores like Wal-Mart began reporting that all their supplies of American flags, usually reserved for holidays like the Fourth of July, were selling out.[24] Millions of Americans began displaying flags—on houses, in yards, on automobiles, and even pinned to lapels or as prints on shirts, shorts, hats, and bathing suits— to express themselves as patriots. The American flag, long an honored symbol in this country, was rediscovered attached to another new symbol post-9/11 when it was attached to the sides of fire engines driving throughout different cities across the country. Even in places of critical introspection about the meaning of terms like *patriotism*—in cities like Berkeley, California—people were engaging in discourse about terrorism by expressing themselves symbolically with the flag.[25]

## ❖ SUMMARY

In this chapter, we have reviewed how our own discourse about public issues like terrorism is influenced and manipulated by public oratory from leaders of the state. To that end, we have explored how important an analysis of the rhetorical audience is for the creation of the oratorical message generally and for terrorism specifically, as well as the ways in which assumptions about the audience(s) influence the message choices the orator will make. We have examined some of the many possible uses of rhetorical figures used in oratory, how they can affect an audience, and how some of the more common intentional uses of rhetorical fallacies manipulate audiences exposed to oratorical addresses. All of this was done to offer you some tools for critical evaluation of public speeches by our government leaders that describe terrorism in this country. Using two dominant public addresses from President Bush about the attacks of September 11, we then employed some of these tools to engage in critical analysis of how his speeches helped shape and, to some degree, limit our discourse about terrorism. To this point, I have provided all of the analysis for using these tools with the president's speeches on terrorism. I would encourage you to read more speeches from President Bush and other leaders addressing terrorism and the attacks of 9/11, this time using the same rhetorical tools (audience analysis, selection of appeals, rhetorical figures, and rhetorical fallacies) to critically evaluate each speech and understand how it affected our discourse.

As you read these, consider the following questions. What assumptions would you make about the audience(s) President Bush addresses? How are rhetorical appeals employed to target this (these) audience(s)? How many figures and fallacies do you find in the speech, and why do you think the speaker is using them? Finally, what impact does this speech have on our discourse about terrorism? Does it extend the effect of the previous speeches, or is there something different in play?

## ❖ NOTES

1. War Powers Act of 1973, Public Law 93-1-48.

2. Section 5(b) of the War Powers Act requires that the president report on military activities to the Congress and adds: "Within sixty calendar days after a report is submitted or required to be submitted . . . the President shall terminate use of U.S. Armed Forces unless the Congress (1) has declared war or has enacted specific authorization for such use of U.S. Armed Forces, (2) has extended by law such sixty day period, (3) is physically unable to meet as a result of an armed attack on the United States."

3. For a complete and thorough description of audience analysis in public speaking and persuasion, see Joseph S. Tuman and Douglas M. Fraleigh, *The St. Martin's Guide to Public Speaking* (New York: St. Martin's Press, 2002), pp. 89–115.

4. Ibid., pp. 97–102.

5. Ibid., pp. 92–3.

6. Ibid., pp. 93–4.

7. Ibid.

8. Ibid., pp. 95–6.

9. Ibid., pp. 102–3.

10. Ibid., pp. 104–5.

11. Ibid., pp. 105–7.

12. See *Texas v. Johnson,* 109 S. Ct. 2533 (1989).

13. E.g., in *Texas v. Johnson,* Chief Justice William Rehnquist, writing a dissenting opinion, offered a historical perspective on the use and meaning of the flag to defend the legality of laws preventing its destruction by burning.

14. This speech was made at a campaign appearance before the Greater Houston Ministerial Association in September 1960. The address, entitled "Religion in Government," gave Kennedy a chance to put the issue of his

religious faith behind him for good. For a text of this speech, see Adrienne Miller, *Rhetorical Theory and Practice* (Berkeley: University of California Press, 1987), pp. 37–9.

15. Ibid., p. 38.

16. The speech, entitled "Let Us Continue," was delivered on November 27, 1963, only 5 days after Kennedy's death. It was as much a speech to the nation and the world as it was an address to the Congress, and it provided everyone a real glimpse of Johnson in an entirely new role, and in a new light in a time of genuine crisis. For a text of this speech, see Theodore Windt, *Presidential Rhetoric*, 5th ed. (Dubuque, IA: Kendall Hunt, 1994), pp. 53–5.

17. This speech was delivered January 20, 1969. For text, see ibid., pp. 123–7.

18. This speech, entitled "Win!" was delivered to a special joint session of the Congress on October 8, 1974, as inflation rates climbed out of control and as many, with serious doubts about the pardoning of Richard Nixon, began to question Ford's ability to lead the nation. For text, see ibid., pp. 242–9.

19. Ibid., p. 244.

20. This 1980 State of the Union address by President Carter is often recalled as the speech that announced the "Carter Doctrine" for American foreign policy. Ibid., p. 297; the full text of the speech is on pp. 296–302.

21. This address, entitled "The Conservative Cause," was made to the Conservative Political Action Committee (an obviously sympathetic audience for Reagan) on February 26, 1982. Ibid., p. 339; the full text of the speech is on pp. 335–42.

22. The concept of a felony murder rule dates all the way back to English common law, and today, all states in the union have a version of this rule, as does the federal government (18 U.S.C. § 1111). The application of such a rule holds that anyone who is involved in the commission of a felony may be held responsible for any death that occurs as a result of the felony. For example, the driver of the getaway car (who him- or herself does not use a weapon or participate directly in an armed robbery) can still be found guilty of first-degree murder if anyone is killed in the commission of the crime. By operating the car, the driver facilitates and aids in the robbery and thus shares in its consequences.

23. E.g., during the horrible violence in Bosnia, NATO members were not of one mind about how (or indeed if) to respond to the conflict.

24. See Will Evans, "Flag Merchants See Little Let-up Since September 11," *Sacramento Bee*, July 3, 2002, which noted that from September 11, 2001, to May 23, 2002, Wal-Mart had sold 4.96 million flags, up from 1.18 million the year before.

25. Merrill Collett, "Old Glory Beckons a Berkeley Peacenik," *Los Angeles Times*, September 24, 2001.

# 6

# Mass-Mediated Images and Construction of Terrorism

To this point, we have considered how terrorism can be rhetorical by examining the defining and labeling of terror as a rhetorical act; the symbolic messages in terror violence, means, and targets; and the public rhetorical discourse about terror. A final, equally significant factor to consider is the way this rhetoric is to some degree preconditioned in the minds of different audiences by images and representations in mass media. Without the assistance of media, terrorist rhetoric would influence only those in the immediate vicinity of terrorist violence and destruction. Conversely, with the assistance of media, terrorism reaches a much broader, sometimes global audience—and in an era in which most people (at least in the United States) get their political information from television, mass-mediated depictions of terrorism can have a profound effect upon the way we think about and engage in discourse about terrorism. Political science professor Abraham Miller once noted:

> Terrorism and the media are entwined in an almost inexorable, symbiotic relationship. Terrorism is capable of writing any drama—no matter how horrible—to compel the media's attention. . . . Terrorism, like an ill-mannered *enfant terrible,* is the

media's stepchild, a stepchild which the media, unfortunately, can neither completely ignore nor deny.[1]

Though Miller was really describing a relationship between *news* media and terrorism, I would expand his claim and suggest that the same can be said about the relationship of all mass media with terrorism, including popular/entertainment media.

In this chapter, we will examine how this relationship operates and how it affects our precepts and discourse about terrorism. To that end, we will consider what mass media are, how entertainment media are different from news media, and how broadcast media (television and radio) are different from print media (newspapers and magazines). We will also examine how public perceptions about terrorism are primed by representations of terrorists in entertainment media like popular cinema and genre literature. In exploring the connection between news media and terrorism, we will consider how terrorists and news media share in a symbiotic, mutually exploitative relationship; how public discourse about terrorism is also primed by mediated images of terrorists and terror violence in broadcast and (to a lesser degree) print news media; and how terrorists have learned to manipulate news media to ensure publication and distribution of their rhetoric to a global audience.

❖  UNDERSTANDING MASS MEDIA

Before we can explore how the relationship between terrorism and media works, we would be well served to define exactly what is meant by the term *mass media*. Richard Campbell, director of the School of Journalism at Middle Tennessee State University, has described mass media as "the cultural industries—the channels of communication—that produce and distribute songs, novels, newspapers, movies, internet services, and other cultural products to large numbers of people."[2] Framed in this light, mass media can be seen as a conduit through which information about culture is transmitted to potentially sizable audiences. Campbell's definition is useful for our discussion because it references mass media from multiple perspectives: entertainment media and news media, print and broadcast media, and digital and film media. The information about culture that is transmitted via this conduit includes all symbols of expression that individuals, groups, and societies use to make sense of their lives and to articulate values and ideals.[3] Though all of these channels of communication may be folded into our concept of mass media generally, they are all different and distinct from one another. *Entertainment media*—which can include fiction books and short stories, cinema, and television programs such as situation comedies, episodic and action dramas, and even televised sports contests, "real-life" programming, and game shows—are different from *news media*, which include newspapers and magazines, journals, Internet sites, and broadcast and cable news. How are they different?

To begin with, what I have described above as entertainment media function primarily to entertain or provide escape and recreation for their audiences. As it had always been with theater, literature, and popular fiction, and as it continues to be with television entertainment and cinema, these channels of media are not necessarily designed to be factual or literal in their interpretation of events or storytelling. Even when addressing real-world events and issues—as can be seen with reality-based television shows like the still-popular *Survivor* program, or with movies based on real events such as director Wolfgang Peterson's *The Perfect Storm* (adapted from Sebastian Junger's book, which describes a real-life storm)—it is implicitly understood that what is presented as reality will have been modified to package the broadcast or film as entertainment. For reality-based programs like *Survivor*, this packaging begins with the careful selection of contestants as a cast, the fallacious presentation of what appears to be a remote and isolated location, the crafting of special contests for games, and the presence of cameras to record what seems like every thought and word and action by contestants. Even with these modifications, not all video shot for *Survivor* makes it into the broadcasting program. Editing choices are made about what to put in and what to leave out—and in what order—to make the story about the contest more entertaining.

Similarly, in films like *The Perfect Storm*, which are said to be "based upon" or "inspired by" real-life events—a certain amount of license is employed by the filmmaker to make the story more compelling.[4] Whether that takes the form of adding or deleting characters, changing time lines or locales, or even altering the focus of conflict in the story, it invariably makes the film a "story" in the fictional sense, and not something to be taken literally.

News media, by contrast, operate under an admittedly risky assumption that what is presented as news is factual and can be trusted or taken literally. In contemporary America, journalism—the process by which news information is gathered and presented as stories for print or broadcast—has cast itself in the role of providing important information, facts, and ideas to assist citizens in making decisions about their lives and about participating in self-governance for democracy. Print news media (primarily newspapers and magazines, and to a lesser degree, online news sources) and broadcast news media (television news and, to a lesser extent, radio broadcast news) generally operate within the same context of providing necessary information for the public, but the peculiarities of each kind of medium (print vs. broadcast) make for important differences in the way news information is presented and packaged to the public.

Although print media like newspapers must sell advertising to augment subscriptions and remain profitable, the general length of articles and stories can be longer and more in depth than what is frequently presented in a televised or radio broadcast story. Of course, with televised news stories, the necessity for brevity in the actual number of words written and delivered in a story can be compensated for by the visual aspect of the medium: A news reporter's words can be augmented by video footage that communicates an amazing amount of detail to the viewer, even within the limited time of a short televised news story.

It is also true for print media such as newspapers and magazines that what is reported often must trail what actually happens, simply because there must be time allowed to write, edit, and print a story in a publication that comes out late in the day, or the following morning, or the following week. In this way, print news media provide a post facto coverage of news events and stories. By contrast, broadcast news (and to some extent, online news), especially since the advent of CNN and cable television, has the ability to broadcast and tell a story in real time as it is unfolding. Nowadays, this kind of news can be available to a viewing public on a constant 24-hour basis, every day of the year. From on-the-spot reporting and video footage broadcast as an event unfolds, this kind of news medium takes on a credibility similar to the account of an eyewitness to the news story. In fact, often this kind of coverage can make the viewer or listener an eyewitness. Of necessity, the ability to tell a story visually elevates the significance of the visual aspect of the medium. This in turn means that how and if a story may be told visually (with live video or file copy) plays a great role in determining when and if a story will be reported at all. Public relations experts and media consultants understand this aspect of broadcast news and often work to frame events that can be covered visually to help ensure that a story will be broadcast.[5]

Both print and broadcast news media follow another tradition of American journalism by framing stories about important issues in terms of *conflict*. Such conflict can be seen when ideas (e.g., Palestinian statehood vs. Israeli security and sovereignty), entities (e.g., the United States government vs. the government of Iraq) or individuals (candidates in an election campaign) in stories are pitted against one another, creating an illusion of balanced reporting but really generating conflict in order to make the story more compelling. In this way, news media take a cue from entertainment media.

The wonderful writer and thinker Ishmael Reed once told me that all "fiction is friction." By that he meant that the key to writing good fiction stories is in the friction or conflict that can be identified within. This much is true for literature, or theater—or television and cinema. Conflict draws readers and viewers into a story and sustains their interest. And as it is for entertainment, so it becomes for news media. In truth, both fiction and nonfiction need friction.

Interestingly enough, though entertainment and news media differ in many ways, they also share points of *convergence*—both from within a media type (e.g., in entertainment media, when rap stars cross over to making television sitcoms or movies), and in between media types (e.g., when news media stories cross over and become entertainment media, like books or movies). In this way, a series of newspaper stories in the *Washington Post* about the Watergate break-in can later become a best-selling nonfiction book (*All the President's Men*), which later crosses over and becomes an Oscar-winning movie with Dustin Hoffman, Robert Redford, and Jason Robards acting in the title roles. The focus of conflict that is common to both entertainment and news media allows for this convergence, as does the fact that being a high-profile story, author, or performer in one kind of medium can help generate popularity for a work that appears in a different medium.[6]

Understanding how mass media may be divided between entertainment and news media and how these may also be further segmented between print and broadcast media offers a useful place for continuing our discussion of the relationship between mass media and terrorism. In the following section, we will develop a description of this relationship, beginning with how terrorism *from above* and *from below* approaches mass media in different ways. As we continue in this discussion, we will consider how framing conflict and the possibility of convergence factor into mass-mediated images of terrorism.

## ❖  TERRORISM FROM ABOVE AND MASS MEDIA

As suggested at the beginning of this chapter, terrorism and mass media share a symbiotic relationship of sorts, with each being dependent on the other for benefits and resources. The nature of this symbiosis depends in no small measure upon whether the terrorism described is *from above* or *from below*. Most of the research documenting a relationship between terrorism and mass media has presumed a nonstate, dissent model, previously referenced as terrorism *from below*. Being allowed to communicate a message to a larger audience helps guarantee potentially greater significance and impression for the message. On occasion, this can legitimate the message or the messenger; at other times, it may lead to a lack of public sympathy for the terrorist or his or her cause. By contrast, media benefit from this relationship, for terrorist activities also help generate viewer and reader interest, ensuring an even larger audience. In the remaining portion of this chapter, we will focus on some of this research and explore how rhetorical messages in terrorism are constructed via manipulation of and by mass media in the realm of both entertainment and news media.

For the time, however, it is important to also distinguish examples of terror *from above,* exploring how this kind of terrorism also has a symbiotic relationship of sorts with mass media, from which benefits and resources can be realized by the state. How these benefits are derived in turn depends upon whether the state in question has eliminated or strictly controls mass media or operates a propaganda and public relations effort with a basically free mass media.

For example, the Communist Khmer Rouge, which ruled the country of Cambodia from 1975 to 1979, practiced terrorism on its own people, including the use of mass murder, torture, starvation, forced relocation, forced labor, and destruction and/or confiscation of personal property. Estimates of the number of people killed by the Khmer Rouge have routinely been placed at 1.7 million out of a population of 8 million people—although these numbers may be as high as 2.2 to 2.5 million out of 8 million.[7] In such a repressive environment, there was no press or media as we understand it today—only the propaganda of the party. As such, it is difficult even to this day, nearly a quarter-century later, to have accurate records and documentation about what happened. The absence of news media, which might have been critical of the party, or at least might have documented its activities, benefited the Khmer Rouge by ensuring little or no opposition from within Cambodia, only opposition from outside after the fact.

In countries and societies allowing for different kinds of mass media but exerting strict government control of either entertainment or news, there are similar benefits to a lack of critique or opposition to state terrorism, and resources to be gained by the state from sponsorship of propaganda. For example, the German National Socialist Party—the Nazis—under Adolph Hitler as leader and Josef Goebbels as Minister of Propaganda, ruthlessly subjugated its own people and eventually terrorized the rest of Europe, resulting in the deaths of millions. Though the Nazis were not very successful in using mass media to persuade countries outside Germany that conditions in Europe justified Nazi advances,[8] they were extremely successful in using the same propaganda on their own people to all but eliminate opposition to the party and to introduce their own rationalization for the barbarity of their regime. As semantics scholar and former U.S. Senator S. I. Hayakawa once noted:

Anyone or anything that stood in the way of Hitler's wishes was "Jewish," "degenerate," "corrupt," "democratic," "internationalist," and as a crowning insult, "non-Aryan." On the other hand, everything that Hitler chose to call "Aryan" was by definition noble, virtuous, heroic, and altogether glorious.[9]

The same may be said for the former Soviet Union, which under Josef Stalin aggressively used state-sponsored propaganda to justify the existence of the Soviet Communist Party,[10] while also muting any mention or criticism of the fact that Stalin was responsible for the deaths, torture, persecution, and forced relocation of millions of his own people. The Soviet Union that survived Stalin, though perhaps not as openly repressive, nevertheless pursued an equally directive relationship with the state news agency, Tass, which presented the official Soviet view of news, while also muting and avoiding any criticism of the state's actions.

This was a pattern also followed (and continued to this day) in Communist China, which strictly controls the news media and regulates what kind of entertainment media may be produced from within or imported from outside the country. For decades, China's former leader, Mao Tse-tung, used state news media to try and knit a cohesive message about the glories of the Communist Party, while also being openly critical of anything outside China. This same medium historically did not allow for internal coverage or commentary of anything that might be critical of the government or the party, including any stories about arrests or executions of dissenters. Years after Mao's rule, the state continues to control mass media in China—with some success in events like the uprising at Tiananmen Square in 1989. Many student demonstrators were killed or injured during this uprising, a fact transmitted widely on television outside China but described very differently, if at all, within China. In modern times, however, though the state continues to try to regulate mass media in China, the realities of marketplace competition have meant that more and more quasi-independent news media and entertainment media have begun to challenge the state's control.[11] This competition, along with the advent and spread of the Internet, has provided the opportunity for some lessening in the strength of the state's grip on mass media in China.

For countries that see themselves as open societies with free and democratic governments and little or no restriction of mass media, there are still benefits and resources to be gained from manipulation (if not strict control) of media. Even a democracy may be observed to engage, either by accident or by design, in what some may consider as state terrorism. The United States' historical treatment of Native Americans might fall under such a heading, as might its involvement in My Lai during the Vietnam War, or in any military conflict where innocent civilians are killed or injured, such as the aforementioned episode in Afghanistan in Chapter 3. Likewise, a democratic country like Israel may have its own actions questioned in dealing with a Palestinian uprising, when, in cases like the military response to a rash of suicide bombings in 2002, the Israeli military adopted a policy of using Palestinian neighbors in housing complexes and apartment buildings to identify where terrorists were hiding by having them go (in the place of Israeli soldiers) and knock on the doors of suspected terrorists, on the assumption that the terrorists would not kill their own people. This policy, which resulted in the deaths and injuries of some Palestinians, raised a cry in both Palestine and Israel, including criticism in the Israeli news media. In this case, as has been the pattern with the U.S. government when dealing with similar criticism, the response has not been to censor the media or to limit what can be said. Rather, democratic countries manipulate their messages by practicing public relations (a more politically acceptable term for *propaganda*) by providing their own version of "the facts" for news media, replete with their own briefing sessions, their own supply of experts and authorities to quote, and the time-honored tradition of *spin*. As to the latter of these, media-savvy governments are quick to get their version of a controversial story out in front of the media early in order to try and influence what the story will be rather than being forced to react to what it has become. Though this kind of response pales in comparison to elimination of all media or strict control of state media, it is nevertheless a method of manipulating how mass media present and report messages about terrorism, and it again allows the state to benefit from diminished or little lasting criticism.

## ❖ TERRORISM FROM BELOW AND MASS MEDIA

As mentioned earlier in this chapter, the traditional approach to studying and identifying a relationship between terrorism and mass media has usually focused upon nonstate, dissent terrorism *from below* and its relationship to mass media—really in the form of news media. In this last part of the chapter, I will discuss this relationship for terrorism *from below*, although I will expand the treatment of how this relationship works by also including entertainment media along with news media. To that end, I will address how terrorist stereotypes are engendered by representations in popular entertainment such as movies and books, how mythologizing of specific terrorists can occur in both news and entertainment media, and generally how terrorists can manipulate—and become manipulated by—news media.

### Terrorist Stereotypes and Entertainment Media

It should come as no surprise to the reader that if Ishmael Reed's words about fiction and friction are accurate, terrorism as subject matter and terrorists as character studies should prove an undeniable attraction for storytellers, novelists, and later for filmmakers. Examples of terrorism and terrorists can be found in any number of writings by prominent authors, including Joseph Conrad's *Secret Agent*[12] (dealing with a theme of betrayal within a group of anarchist terrorists), Robert Louis Stevenson and Fanny van de Grift Stevenson's *The Dynamiter*[13] (dealing with a crazed bomber who ends up blowing up an innocent woman's home in the hope it will terrorize all of England), Fyodor Dostoyevsky's *Besy* (translated as *The Devils* or *The Possessed*)[14] (which deals with themes of murder and destruction for their own sake), Liam O'Flaherty's *The Informer*[15] (dealing with themes of betrayal and martyrdom for the terrorist), and, in more recent times, John LeCarré's

*The Little Drummer Girl*[16] (also dealing with a portrait of terrorists, a theme of betrayal, and how law enforcement must use people to catch and kill terrorists).

Though these works of literature have contributed to a growing image of terrorists in different historical contexts, they have not been as widely influential[17] in more modern times as the books of so-called thriller writers, who have mixed genres of crime novels and spy and espionage to develop their newer variation, featuring terrorism as the focus of conflict and terrorists as the new villains to be stopped at all costs. Although the collapse of the Soviet Union and the Iron Curtain created a greater temptation for West-based thriller writers to look to other sources (besides the Soviets or their henchmen in the Eastern Bloc countries) for villains, books featuring terrorists were popular and slowly beginning to affect public perceptions about terrorists and terrorism decades before the breakup of the USSR. Many of these earlier works focused specifically on Middle Eastern terrorism, usually featuring Palestinian terrorists or their Arab allies in the roles of terrorist villains. Fresh with the real-life examples of Middle East terror violence at the 1972 Munich Olympics, or the years of ensuing airline hijackings, terrorist bombings, kidnappings, and assassinations, writers found that thriller books on the same subject could appeal to a wide audience, but only if the premise of the book was in some way more audacious than reality as presented in news media. Bookstore shelves quickly filled with the commercial works of thriller writers focusing upon Middle Eastern terrorism. One audacious and successful example of this was a 1975 book by thriller writer Thomas Harris (the same writer who would later write *The Silence of the Lambs*) in *Black Sunday*,[18] an extremely popular story about Palestinian terrorists who attempt to detonate a bomb carried in the Goodyear blimp as it passes over America's sacred ritual—the Super Bowl. Although today (in a post-9/11 world) the premise for such a book may not appear so outlandish, at the time it did appear that way, and that made for a large part of its commercial success and crossover convergence to Hollywood movie, with the late Robert Shaw in the role of an Israeli intelligence agent who . . . (sorry, you'll have to read the book or rent the video to find out what happens).

In works like Harris's thriller and the film adaptation of the same, however, a disturbing stereotype of the terrorist as Arab began to emerge. This individual was a fanatic, fiercely anti-Semitic, passionate about his or her cause but without empathy for the humans who become sacrificed, a cold-blooded killer, and, in the end, something less than a human being. Unlike LeCarré's complex characters or the morally ambiguous characters presented by Conrad or Dostoyevsky, these characters were mostly one-dimensional stereotypes, from their wooden dialogue to the cliché descriptions of their appearance or personal habits.

Similar depictions, even if less significant by their numbers, began to appear of other terrorist groups—most prominently Irish terrorists and Latin or South American terrorists. Books such as William Granger's *November Man*[19] (dealing with the real-life murder of Louis Mountbatten by Irish terrorists) and later work by techno-thriller writer Tom Clancy in *Patriot Games*[20] (dealing with IRA plots for assassination and revenge against British and, later, American targets) suggested more one-dimensional views of the terrorist as an Irish fanatic, quasi-alcoholic, cold-blooded killer—whether male or female. A later Clancy book, *Clear and Present Danger*,[21] dealt with the relationship of terrorist violence and narcotics trade in Colombia. In this second book, Clancy suggested an image of the modern narco-terrorist as a cross between zealous fanatic, ardent nationalist, and stereotypical drug lord/thug.

Though these books have had some impact on large commercial audiences in preconditioning (or reinforcing) stereotypes about terrorists and terrorism, a more prominent source of stereotyping has been the movie versions and adaptations of these same stories—or those of original screenplays (is there such a thing as an original screenplay?) for action/thriller movies. The following are some more contemporary examples of films that, like the books discussed above, stereotype individuals as terrorists and simplify terrorist causes.

In 1994, Hollywood director James Cameron wrote and directed Arnold Schwarzenegger in *True Lies,* a story about international intrigue, Middle East terrorism, a plot to detonate a nuclear device in Florida—and (of all things!) marital infidelity, the latter of which explains the film's title. A huge hit at the box office, *True Lies* also created considerable controversy for its stereotyping of Arabs as terrorists.[22] Fearing just such a backlash, Cameron pointed to the inclusion of a sympathetic and humorous Arab sidekick character for Schwarzenegger. As played by actor Grant Heslov, the sympathetic or good Arab character is Schwarzenegger's "computer nerd," named Faisal. Critics, however, weren't swayed. Faisal's role is minor and plays like a token character when contrasted against the villainous bad Arab terrorists. The main terrorist villain in *True Lies* is Salim Abu Aziz, also nicknamed the "Sand Spider" to make him appear more ominous. As played by veteran actor Art Malik (who also appears forever type-cast), he leads a large army of Arab terrorists of nondescript origin, linked together by what the movie calls the "Crimson Jihaad." Ironically, in many of the early scenes of the film, the actors playing Faisal the good Arab and Aziz the bad Arab actually physically resemble one another, although, as the film progresses, Aziz's character slides into the more typical stereotype of Arab terrorists. As presented, Aziz and his men are sexist, violent brutes and religious fanatics; they have more money than they know what to do with, and they are fiercely anti-American. Most possess exaggerated Arab features—dark skin, oily hair, and thick beards or unshaven faces—and they dress in paramilitary clothing baggy enough to barely conceal large automatic weapons, even when casually strolling the streets of Washington, D.C. To make the stereotype complete, they are also extremely incompetent.

*True Lies* contrasts with another film, released in 1996, called *Executive Decision.* As produced by veteran action filmmaker Joel Silver, *Executive Decision* featured Kurt Russell as a think tank expert named Dr. Grant (a role perilously close to Tom Clancy's Jack Ryan character), who teams with Steven Seagal to stop a group of fanatical Arab terror-ists who have seized a commercial airline jet en route to Washington, D.C. The terrorists are led by a character called Nagi Hassan, and early in the films we see him reading from the Koran and praying, so that there can be no doubt that he is Muslim. As played by actor David Suchet, Hassan's character pretends to want to exchange hostages on the plane for an imprisoned terrorist colleague, but in reality, he has packed the airline with nerve toxin bought on the black market from the old Soviet Union, and he intends to crash it into the nation's capital, using the jet as the delivery vehicle. Like the characters in *True Lies,* the terrorists in *Executive Decision* are portrayed as religious fanatics, misogynists, and brutal thugs who have plenty of money to finance their operations (presumably because oil-rich Arab states have financed their activity). Again, the cast of Arabs possess exaggerated physical features like dark skin, thick beards or unshaven faces, shaggy clothing, and poor grooming. Once more, they are also presented as hugely incompetent. These stereotypes are really no different, however, from those of countless other depictions of Arabs in films stretching back more than a century.[23]

These stereotypes of Arab terrorists can also be compared with Hollywood depictions of other groups—most prominently, Irish and

South American terrorists. For example, in the 1992 film *Patriot Games*, adapted from the Tom Clancy book of the same name, Harrison Ford plays Dr. Jack Ryan, a scholar and CIA analyst, who inadvertently foils a ULA (Ulster Liberation Army) plot to assassinate members of Great Britain's royal family. Ryan's success in foiling their assassination attempt triggers a campaign of revenge against Ryan's family (his wife and daughter) on American soil, and later, once more, against the same royal family member, played by Edward Fox. The Irish terrorists, Sean Miller and Kevin (as played by Sean Bean and Patrick Bergin), are presented as one-dimensional stereotypes of Irish people generally and Irish terrorists specifically. They are portrayed as radical zealots, myopic in their views about the British, hard drinkers, ruthless killers, and only marginally more competent than the Arab terrorists of the films mentioned above. Bean's character, Sean Miller, is so ruthless, it is mentioned that he once murdered a priest! They are also as willing to kill their fellow terrorists, when it suits their purposes, as they are committed to killing Ryan or the royal family. The latter point is also intended to suggest that they are really committed to nothing except mindless violence. Their physical appearance exaggerates the stereotype: They have pale skin, shaggy, unkempt hair and unshaven beards, and baggy clothing, and they keep alcohol always close at hand. Their image is contrasted in the film with that of another Irishman, played by veteran actor Richard Harris, who appears to have no conscience about Irish terrorist violence but who helps Ryan to avoid the negative publicity that may come from extending this terrorism to America. His character assumes that such bad publicity will hurt Irish American fundraising to assist the IRA or other groups in Ireland. Thus, Harris's character does the right thing but for the wrong reasons.

These films can also be contrasted with another film vehicle for action star Schwarzenegger, the movie *Collateral Damage*, released in 2002 to no small share of controversy. This film had been scheduled for release in the fall of 2001, but the release was delayed because of fear over public backlash given the subject matter. In this film, Schwarzenegger stars as a Los Angeles-based firefighter whose wife and young son are killed by a terrorist bombing. Though not the primary target, his family was nevertheless caught in the same violent explosion. In the words of a character in the movie (mouthing the oft-repeated euphemism used by terrorists and even our own military spokespeople), these innocent victims were so much "collateral damage." Engaging in more than a bit of fantasy even by Hollywood standards,

Schwarzenegger's character departs on a journey of revenge, taking him into the heart of Colombia in search of the drug-trafficking Colombian terrorist leader Claudio Perrini, as played by actor Cliff Curtis. Claudio, who is initially suggested to be the nefarious El Lobo ("The Wolf"),[24] and his fellow narco-terrorists are depicted slightly differently from Arab and Irish terrorists in other Hollywood films. Here, they are given uniforms and natty berets—suggesting some kind of army—but again they have dark skin, long oily hair, and beards, and they live in general squalor as they protect their drug trade and plan their next terror mission. El Lobo's reason for bombing a building in America is to pay back the United States for military assistance to the Colombian government in the war on drugs. Again, a stereotype of the South American—and specifically Colombian—terrorist emerges. Terrorists there are also drug traffickers. Their uniforms suggest a past connection to revolution, most likely sponsored once upon a time by Cuba or the Soviet Union. They are also bloodthirsty killers without conscience. In one scene of violence—ostensibly placed for no other purpose than to emphasize how psychopathic Claudio is—Perrini tortures one of his own men, forcing a poisonous snake down his throat and watching as the man suffers a slow and agonizing death. Claudio's treachery pales, however, next to that of his wife—the real El Lobo—who connives to use a child to carry a second bomb into a federal building to kill more CIA and State Department officials.

The forcefulness of the stereotypes employed in these films can be better appreciated when they are all, in turn, compared with another Hollywood blockbuster, starring Bruce Willis and dealing with the taking of hostages in a building in Los Angeles. The 1988 film *Die Hard*—itself a mix of disaster genre films like *Towering Inferno* and police/action films of previous decades—served up a template for many films that would follow, depicting terrorism and lone heroes.[25] In this film by director John McTiernan, Willis plays a New York police officer on vacation to visit his estranged wife at Christmas. As he reaches her place of business in Los Angeles—a monolithic building called the Nakatomi Tower—a group of armed men takes the building, claiming all inhabitants as hostages. Willis spends the balance of the movie without shoes, running through broken glass, smoking cigarettes, making wisecracks, and shooting villains. These men are led by Hans Gruber, played by Alan Rickman, who initially makes pronouncements about the "greed" of the company whose building he has taken and makes other passing references to "Arafat" or the need to "teach a lesson," suggesting that he and his men are what they appear to be: terrorists. Shortly thereafter, however, they remove one of the hostages and isolate him, demanding that he give up a security code to allow them access to their real objective: a company vault containing $600 million in negotiable bearer bonds. The hostage exclaims in surprise: "You want money? *What kind of terrorists are you?*" Gruber laughs and replies: "Who said we were terrorists?" Although this was director McTiernan's nod to the audience that not all things are what they appear, Gruber's rhetorical question is not as surprising as it sounds. From the moment these men appear on screen, they do some of the things we associate with terrorism, but their appearance and dialogue and ultimate actions have already cued the audience that something is amiss here. They do not fit the stereotype of the terrorists in other films mentioned above. These men are handsome, tall, strong, focused, articulate, well educated, and (with two exceptions) distinctly German. With long, carefully brushed hair, a fashionable wardrobe that includes rock star leather pants for some and Savile Row suits for another, they could as easily have fit in at a trendy restaurant in Santa Monica or Beverly Hills. Although the promotional literature for *Die Hard* describes Gruber and his men as terrorists, the audience (already preconditioned to see terrorists as something different) knows them for what they are: elegant criminals.

When considered in this light, the impact of stereotyping specific groups as terrorists by their inclusion in literature, popular fiction, and, most significantly, Hollywood movies helps to precondition a belief or expectation in any audience member that certain kinds of people and terrorists are indeed one and the same. Can there be any mystery about the fact that Middle East terrorists were initially suspected in the Oklahoma City bombing, well before anyone in the law enforcement community connected the act of terrorism to Timothy McVeigh?[26] This is not to suggest that books and movies alone are responsible for such preconceptions. But this kind of mass media representation of terrorism exerts a powerful influence on how we see and understand terrorists. This influence, however, must itself be contextualized in the ways mass media mythologize—or are used to mythologize—terrorism and how terrorists interact with news media.

## Mythologizing Terrorism in News and Entertainment Media

One of the reasons that stereotypes about terrorists have influence on our discourse about terrorism is because of the presence of mass-mediated myths about terrorist groups and individuals.[27] Myths are fabrications crafted from analysis and ideas of half or partial truths. As fabrications, they become exaggerations or morph into claims that have little basis in fact. When employed in popular culture, however, they can have lasting impact on public beliefs and discourse. In the context of terrorism, simple yet damaging myths support stereotypes such as those referenced above for Arabs, the Irish, and South Americans. For example, there is a myth that all Arabs are Muslim. In truth, many Arabs may be Muslim, but many are also Christian. Moreover, Islam as a religion reaches nearly half the world's population, including people around the planet. There is also a myth about Arabs suggesting they are rich with oil money—although the reality is that only some countries with Arab populations have oil resources, and even within these countries, the wealth generated by the sale of oil is not shared by all in the population. Nevertheless, these myths about Arabs support the stereotypes of Arab terrorists as always being Muslim and having their activities always financed with oil money.

Some myths also contain the potential to become stories, reinforcing the same stereotypes but also with the capacity to make something—or someone—larger than life. In the context of terrorism, two examples of mythology constructed within news and entertainment media suffice to illustrate this point.

Earlier, in Chapter 4, I discussed the historical origins of the American Ku Klux Klan, emphasizing that what we understand as the Klan today is actually the product of three different incarnations of this group, the second of which occurred at the beginning of the past century. It was in this period that a book by Thomas Dixon appeared, recasting the history of Reconstruction in the South as told from the perspective of heroic Southerners. Dixon himself had been born in North Carolina and educated at Wake Forest College before graduate school at Johns Hopkins. As a young man, he had lived through the Reconstruction era he would later depict, first in *The Leopard's Spots*, published in 1902, and then in *The Clansman, An Historic Romance of the Ku Klux Klan*, published in 1905. Though the first of these books had been well received, the latter of these (referred to as *The Clansman* for brevity) was a strong commercial success. *The Clansman* tells the story of a young ex-Confederate colonel named Ben Cameron who is taken care of in a prison hospital by Elsie Stoneman—who turns out to be the sister of Cameron's captor, and chief foil, Phil Stoneman. Ben and Elsie fall in love. Phil Stoneman, in turn, falls in love with Cameron's sister—but much of this love story/metaphor for reconciliation of North and South is thwarted when Phil and Elsie's father—a Congressman Stoneman—enters the story, determined to force Reconstruction on the South and use Negroes as his tools. The Negroes of Dixon's story are not sympathetic characters; they are ignorant, savage, brutish, and degenerate. It is up to Cameron, as the Grand Dragon of the Ku Klux Klan, to save the South from Negroes and Reconstruction, in a way suggesting the Klan as a noble group of honor-bound men protecting tradition and civilization. Naturally, Dixon's historical revision takes great license with facts. As suggested in Chapter 4, the origins of the Klan did include the membership of ex-Confederate officers who fancied themselves honorable gentlemen. The historical record of the original Klan also documents that any nobility of purpose in the Klan quickly dissipated as its members became more openly violent and vigilantelike.

Here, popular fiction helped create a mythology of the Klan—a terrorist organization—promoting it as something more noble and acceptable. This representation of the terrorist group then went through a kind of media convergence, as D. W. Griffith purchased the rights to the story and set out to make a historic epic film that would later be retitled *The Birth of a Nation*. While keeping the roots of Dixon's story intact, Griffith added new and untried cinematic advances, including sweeping panoramic shots, different forms of closeup shots for contrast, and a huge and rich orchestral score that emotionally charged the epic historical/love story. Though *The Birth of a Nation* was not without its detractors, it did enjoy immense commercial success. Full-house audiences were willing to pay as much as a whopping $2 to see the film, and it grossed nearly $18 million in box office revenue before moving on to art house theaters.

It was in no small measure the result of the success of the book and later the film (the latter of which reached an admittedly larger audience) that the myth of the old Klan grew, transforming its reputation from one of racist and vicious thugs to one of noble and responsible gentlemen who only wanted to preserve what was best about the old South. When the Klan thus went through its aforementioned second incarnation under the guidance of Colonel Simmons, it was the existence of this myth, as developed through mass-mediated convergence of book and cinema, that allowed the new group to be seen as nothing more than a service club and a fraternal organization, devoted to civic service. Such a myth allowed the membership ranks of the new Klan to swell well into the millions. Only the reporting of years of savage and violent activity by the Klan—now directed against unionists, immigrants, Catholics, and Jews as well as blacks—along with reporting of financial improprieties—would again restore the public perception of the Klan as a group of racist and bigoted vigilantes/terrorists.

In this first example of mythology and terrorism, a mass-mediated mythology was developed outside the direction of the terrorist group—although the same group was quick to derive benefits and resources from this interaction. In a second example, I will now discuss how the individual terrorist known as Carlos the Jackal enjoyed similar benefits from the mythology constructed around his identity, although in his case, it is clear that he had a direct hand in developing the myth.

Ilich Ramirez Sanchez was the son of a well-to-do lawyer from Venezuela named Jose Altagracia Ramirez Navas. His father, an ardent Marxist, had named his son Ilich in honor of his favorite Bolshevik, Vladimir Ilich Ulynov, also known as Vladimir Ilich Lenin. As the first child and eldest son of Ramirez Navas, Ilich was raised in a relatively pampered environment (compared to his countrymen), yet he also learned much of the Marxist doctrine his father believed in, along with the history of South American revolution. As a teenager, his father sent him abroad, first to study in London and later to attend the Patrice Lumumba University, a Soviet university designed for children of the ruling class in many of the Soviet Union's Third World client states. Here, Ramirez Sanchez met and interacted with Palestinian students, some of whom were connected to the Popular Front for the Liberation of Palestine (PFLP). Some of them introduced him to Wadi Haddad, who, along with George Habash, had been instrumental in helping to start Palestinian terrorism against Israel. Ramirez Sanchez became smitten with their cause, or perhaps romanticized the idea of being a revolutionary, and decided to attend a military training camp for foreign students interested in helping the PFLP.

Thus began his transformation from pampered and spoiled, slightly lazy university student into the terrorist that would remain in the headlines and on the most-wanted lists of international law enforcement agencies for decades. In that period of time, Sanchez would become known by his *nom de guerre* Carlos and would become involved in a series of high-profile bombings, assassinations, hostage takings, and hijackings. These episodes of terror violence included the bombing of several French newspaper offices, the tossing of hand grenades into a crowded area at the Drug Store St. Germain in Paris, rocket attacks on Israeli airliners, the murders of a fellow terrorist-turned-informer along with his two French DST security agents, and the kidnapping for ransom of several OPEC ministers at the OPEC offices in Vienna. It was at the last of these that Carlos communicated to the press through a mediator: "Tell them I'm from Venezuela and my name is Carlos. Tell them I'm the famous Carlos. They know me."[28] By this, Carlos meant to convey that because of his reputation for ruthlessness, the authorities should expect that he would kill hostages if he said he would kill hostages. But it was at this time that Carlos also discovered how much he enjoyed being notorious—as well as noteworthy. Communicating to the authorities in a public way (with the assistance of the media), Carlos would eventually demand and receive a jet to fly both himself and his colleagues and hostages throughout the Middle East before collecting a ransom and eventually escaping in Dar Al Beida Airport, outside Algiers. While still in the bus to the airport in Vienna, Carlos waved at reporters and their cameras, behaving like someone who felt comfortable in the limelight. On the flight, he reportedly handed out autographs, trying to present himself as a modern Robin Hood.[29]

The OPEC terror operation gave Carlos an international reputation and demonstrated how the news media (covering every aspect of the hostage drama) could be manipulated to project his act of terror, while also beginning the process of mythologizing his identity as an outrageous but successful terrorist. Media coverage also took note of hostage descriptions of him as well dressed and groomed, multilingual, and seemingly well educated. To this were added reports of his fondness for the opposite sex.

Over time, media reports would be quick to claim that Carlos was responsible for any terror attack, directly or indirectly. Carlos was now also called by an additional name, *the Jackal*, because a reporter from the London-based *Guardian* newspaper had found, among other things in a London flat rented by Carlos, a copy of thriller writer Frederick Forsyth's novel *The Day of the Jackal*.[30] The news media would openly speculate about whether Carlos had been reading the book and had perhaps left it behind to intentionally influence news coverage of him. That this would later prove false (the book reportedly belonged to the owner of the flat) did not matter; from that point forward, another mass-mediated convergence took place. Between news accounts of the legendary Carlos and news accounts labeling him with the title character of a best-selling thriller novel, Carlos became *the Jackal*.

The following years led to more media convergence as Carlos the Jackal became the focus of numerous fiction books. For example, Robert Ludlum, whose thriller books reached more than 100 million copies worldwide before his recent death, wrote what became one of his biggest best-sellers in *The Bourne Identity*[31] in 1980. Here, Ludlum fictionalized a story of Jason Bourne, an American agent with a constructed identity as the world's top assassin, designed to lure out the legendary Carlos the Jackal in an effort to capture or kill him. To make the media convergence all the more complete (if not confusing!), Ludlum even opened his book by reprinting actual articles from the *New York Times* and the Associated Press, dealing with the exploits of Carlos and helping to bring his now-mythic reputation as a well-dressed ladies' man, ruthless killer, and master of disguise to a full boil. Carlos was James Bond as a terrorist. Ludlum did not allow Carlos to be caught or killed in *The Bourne Identity* and brought him back again in a sequel.[32] A made-for-television miniseries of *The Bourne Identity* helped complete the media convergence, and Hollywood movie treatments followed suit, though not using Carlos by name. In one example of the latter, a 1981 film called *Nighthawks,* starring Sylvester Stallone and Billy Dee Williams as New York cops on an antiterrorist task force, dealt with their efforts to stop a notorious terrorist named Wulfgar, played by Rutger Hauer. Hauer's character, obviously modeled after Carlos, was in New York to kidnap and hold hostage representatives from the United Nations. The plot line was derivative of Carlos and the hostage taking at the OPEC headquarters in Vienna.

These acts of mass-mediated convergence and mythologizing helped Carlos enjoy a global reputation while also putting fear into the public. That many of his later years were spent actually on the run and in hiding, or that he would be captured in 1994 as a pudgy, middle-aged man, in humiliating fashion by French DST agents working in Sudan, seemed to matter little when these facts were placed against his myth. Carlos derived bravado from his mythology during his very public trial in Paris for the murder of the fellow terrorist/informant and the two DST agents. Although assisted by counsel, he defended himself before ultimately being convicted. The release of the movie version of the *Bourne Identity* in the summer of 2002 featured an adaptation of Ludlum's story, minus Carlos the Jackal. With the real middle-aged, pudgy Carlos languishing in prison, featuring and mythologizing him on screen no longer made sense.

### Manipulation of and by News Media

Though mass-mediated stereotypes precondition public assumptions about terrorism, and these stereotypes in turn can be reinforced by terrorist mythology, the most effective opportunity for terrorists themselves to really control and manipulate mediated coverage of their messages resides in the interaction they have with news media. Paradoxically, this is also the place where news media have the ability to manipulate how and if terrorists communicate their message. To understand this paradox, I will first reexamine how news media are attracted to stories they consider newsworthy and how terrorism has been influenced by a desire for media coverage. I will then consider how a modern terrorist interacts with the news media in much the same fashion as a political candidate, with interviews and press conferences, as well as the selective use of videotaped messages for broadcast.

As suggested at the beginning of this chapter, mass media in the form of news media are often drawn (like entertainment media in books or movies) to stories that suggest conflict and the potential for what is shocking and sensational. Mainstream news media, of course, filter these requirements of conflict and the sensational through an initial requirement that a story also be of public interest. Stories describing terror violence almost always meet these requirements, for the violence first and foremost threatens public safety (thereby making it of public interest) and showcases conflict between terrorists and their target audience(s) in a manner that is increasingly dramatic and sensational.

As M. Cherif Bassioni, a recognized expert on international criminal law, has argued, this paradox has created a situation in which terrorists are drawn to news media coverage because they desire maximum publicity for their messages, while media coverage of terrorism magnifies the threat and resulting fear of terrorism to the public.[33] The desire for maximum publicity, in turn, creates a tendency in terrorist violence to select targets and engage in types of symbolic action that translate well visually in coverage and broadcast. *Translating well* means that the violence is a dramatic form of spectacle—something engaging enough to make a viewer stop and take notice.

Though terrorists may feel they are manipulating media in selecting targets for this purpose and engaging in sensational violence to ensure coverage, the opposite is actually true. In a world with media saturation, and news stories already devoted to coverage of so many issues relating to violence, death, and tragedy, guaranteeing coverage of a terrorism story requires visually compelling, dramatic, and therefore devastating violence on a larger and larger scale; sadly, this also means that with each act of terror, the threshold for what is dramatic and truly terrifying must be raised. To put the case plainly, if you kidnap three missionaries in the Philippines and demand that the government release rebel leaders, you might get a print news story and some local coverage. If you detonate a bomb at an embassy or in a public market, killing hundreds and injuring more, you will get more attention from print and broadcast news media.

Palestinian terrorists learned this lesson in the early 1970s. Though they had not been the first to hijack planes as a means of terrorism to draw media attention, they did learn that media coverage would be acute if several planes were hijacked and subsequently blown up. This they did at Dawson's Field in Jordan, in September 1970, while holding a press conference and in the full view of journalists and with cameras running. The resulting spectacle, which was watched by people around the world, only served to raise the bar or standard for what would be considered sensationalized, violent terrorism.

Terrorist groups also learned that manipulation of media could be achieved if they approached news reporters acting less like terrorists and more like politicians or public relations experts. To that end, some terrorists discovered the advantages of selective access to information— a regular tactic of political candidates seeking favorable media coverage. By granting interviews to some but not all reporters as individuals, or newspapers or television networks as entities, terrorists could hold out the promise of a competitive scoop while also guaranteeing coverage and possibly more favorable treatment in a story.[34]

In a similar vein, Ted Kaczynski, the so-called Unabomber, left a trail of murders, attacks, and bombings over 17 years (from 1978 to 1995), killing three people and injuring 29 others, creating a sense of national hysteria, and making many university professors uneasy about receiving and opening their mail. Kaczynski once offered certain news organizations unlimited access to what he called his "manifesto," a complete statement of his political philosophy, but only if they agreed to publish it in its entirety. The *New York Times* and the *Washington Post* took him up on his offer, sparking a national debate about journalist ethics and manipulation by terrorists.

## ❖ TERRORISM AND PAID MEDIA

More recently, terrorist groups have become sophisticated about controlling messages for broadcast and distribution. Like political candidates who use *paid media,* as in political advertising, to guarantee that a message gets out to the public, some terrorists have resorted to producing their own videos for selective release to news entities, in the understanding that such material will be broadcast to a larger audience. The use of this video can have different effects for the multiple audiences it reaches.

For example, in early October 2001, only weeks after the September 11 attacks on the United States, Al Jazeera television, a small and rapidly influential news channel operating in the tiny nation of Qatar, broadcast the first of what would become several exclusive videotapes of Osama bin Laden. Al Jazeera's exclusive prize scooped all other news media entities, forcing them to *re*broadcast what had already been broadcast with credit to the small news station. Many would complain that Al Jazeera was becoming a pawn for bin Laden and his al Qaeda organization,[35] but others correctly observed that the very same video was being broadcast intact by all major Western television news media[36] feeding off the initial broadcast from Al Jazeera. Indeed, CNN was eventually compelled to make an interim arrangement with Al Jazeera, offering to exchange resources for news stories for a chance to get the same exclusives the small station was getting.

Over time, numerous videos were released, and most were aired. The bin Laden tapes, while shot in a style suggesting an amateur working with a simple video camera, were actually fairly sophisticated rhetorical artifacts. Intended not only for his Arab audience in the Middle East—a fact suggested by his speeches in Arabic and his choice of Al Jazeera as the news station for broadcast—these tapes also targeted a larger global audience, including the United States, her allies, and those neutral countries President Bush had warned in his speeches.

The imagery within each tape was compelling. In one tape, as shown in Photo 6.1a, bin Laden is shown at what appears to be a meal, perhaps at a wedding reception for a family member. For Western audiences, the tape at first glance appears to depict a normal meal and celebration. But slower frame-by-frame analysis, as shown in Photo 6.1b, shows that bin Laden is acutely aware of where the camera is and how he appears in it. The event is clearly staged to depict normalcy in his life, as well as a seeming indifference to the threats of a coming military action from President Bush in response to the attacks of 9/11.

In another tape, bin Laden is shown standing with his close collaborator, Al-Zawahri, in what appears to be a training camp for al Qaeda fighters. Of note here is the way that bin Laden and

**Photo 6.1a**    This still, taken from video later broadcast on all news outlets around the world, begins by showing bin Laden in a normal meeting, with an aide and a friend, getting ready to be seated for a meal. The approach looks like a home video.

Al-Zawahri are dressed in white, with open robes, and standing comfortably among so many armed men, whose own faces are concealed beneath wrapped scarves.

The image created by their appearance suggests an attitude of open indifference and defiance to the United States. It is also here that a certain gentleness in bin Laden's demeanor comes across. He does not appear angry or visually fanatical—both characteristics that a viewer would expect given his reputation, history, and rhetoric in other videos. But here, as in later videos, he exudes a sense of calm that communicates either inner strength or a false sense of confidence. Both possibilities make the video in some way more frightening for a global audience, while perhaps giving solace to the Arab audience he wants to inspire.

In a later, now famous video, he appears before what seems to be a cave entrance with a gun at his side, holding a microphone as he delivers a vitriolic speech in a relatively calm voice. A partial translation of

**Photo 6.1b**     Frame by frame analysis of the same video, however, reveals that bin Laden knows exactly where the camera is.

his words, warning of an apocalyptic religious conflict between Muslims and non-Muslims, shows him to say: "These events have split the world into two camps: the camp of the believers and the camp of the infidels. It is the duty of every Muslim to make sure that his religion prevails. The winds of faith and the winds of change are blowing against the infidels who occupy the land of the prophet Mohammed, may peace and God's blessing be upon him." Then to the American audience he adds: "To America and its people I say a few words: I swear to God, who raised the sky without pillars, that America and those who live in it will not be able to dream of security until we live it on the ground in Palestine, and before all of the infidel armies leave the land of the Prophet, may peace and God's blessings be upon him."

Again, his voice is soft, and yet confident. There is a disconnect between the harsh rhetoric and threatening tone of his words and the calm appearance of his delivery. This is no accident. This video was intended, like the others, to assert his leadership in the challenge against the United States and Israel, while also continuing to threaten

**Photo 6.2**    This still, lifted from another video shown by news outlets around the world, depicts bin Laden and an aide visiting an al Qaeda training facility. Note how men are dressed, and how this compares with the al Qaeda fighters around them.

Americans by reminding them of September 11, with veiled references to a lack of "security."

Because of his decision to give exclusive access for the tape to Al-Jazeera, bin Laden ensured its broadcast in the Middle East and rebroadcast in other parts of the world. His words were frightening for an American audience already on edge, and the calmness of his demeanor along with the presence of his gun suggested that more of a struggle was coming.

### Terrorism, Codes, and Cues

On occasion, terrorist video messages may more clearly parallel political advertising techniques. In American political advertising, we have often witnessed the use of what Kathleen Hall Jamieson, Dean of the Annenberg School for Communication at the University of

**Photo 6.3**     In this still, taken from another video played on news outlets, Bin Laden speaks directly into the camera, and to his various audiences—including viewers in the United States.

Pennsylvania, calls "codes" and "veiled visual cueing." Found in many kinds of political advertising but especially effective in television advertising, codes are the double meanings of words or other signs and symbols: those meanings that are literal and obvious and those that amount to subtext, the meaning between the lines. Jamieson writes: "Persuaders often leave clues in the form of otherwise inexplicable details, small lapses in generic propriety, minute blunders—all designed to whisper and gently prompt the sensitive susceptible audience to divine subtextual meaning. In swayable audiences, these cues invite code switching—a shift from the explicit to the implicit text."[37] On occasion, this code switching is cued by something visual in the video of the political advertisement. For example, during the 1990 U.S. Senate race in North Carolina, Democratic candidate and former Charlotte Mayor Harvey Gantt faced off against incumbent Senator Jesse Helms and actually led in the polls with 10 days to go in the campaign. Helms then released a series of television ads targeting Gantt for what appeared to be normal campaign issues concerning

**Photo 6.4a**   In this still, taken from a video released to and broadcast by world wide media outlets, a man charges dramatically towards the camera and the viewer on horseback.

abortion and affirmative action. In each of these ads, however, were visual cues to subtextual messages about *race*. Gantt was African American, and each of Helms's ads was used to prime the audience about race and the need to avoid electing a black man to the Senate. Naturally, these cues were subtle (in Jamieson's language, a "whisper"), but whether through slowing down a video of Gantt, replaying something he had said but in the process exaggerating the slurred sound of his voice, or using black and white photos of Gantt, with his skin color altered to make him appear very dark, the cue to race was unmistakable. For those white voters with the unspoken potential for racial prejudice, the ads primed the issue and raised it as a campaign litmus test. After the 10-day period, Helms won reelection, taking back 62% of the white vote in his state.

The same technique may be seen in a final bin Laden video (Photos 6.4a, 6.4b). This video shows bin Laden on horseback, at first galloping toward the camera as if he is charging it and later casually

**Photo 6.4b**    A second still from the same video shows the rider to be
Osama bin Laden. Note that he never conceals his identity,
and in this picture does not appear to be armed.

riding his horse. Here, we may see a more careful form of visual cueing
to the subtextual message. The image here suggests a warrior—although
in this piece, he does not appear armed. He does, however, appear
purposeful and determined.

For Western audiences unfamiliar with the history of Islam or the
more specific controversy in modern Jerusalem over the status of the so-
called Wailing Wall, the sight of bin Laden on horseback conveys only
a strong, determined individual and, in our uniquely American way of
seeing things, the image of a cowboy. But for audiences in the Middle
East conversant with such history and controversy, the symbolism of
this imagery is altogether different. Here, we find the subtextual message
in this video. Many Jews regard the Wailing Wall (HaKotel HaMa'aravi
in Hebrew, or just the "Kotel") as a deeply sacred site for Judaism. It is
considered to be the only surviving remnant of the Second Temple, and
a chance to pray before it has great symbolic meaning for Jews used to
being in a historical state of Diaspora, without homeland. Controlling
access to this wall is one of the reasons—if not the most important of

reasons—that makes Jerusalem a non-negotiable issue for Israel when negotiating with Palestinians.

Conversely, many Muslims also see this wall today as a significant holy place. It is claimed that at this spot, the prophet Mohammed tethered his winged stallion, called al-Burak, shortly before he ascended to heaven. This story is also called the *Night Journey and Ascension of Mohammed* and has been retold many times, inspiring more literature than even that addressing the miracles of his birth.[38]

Many Israelis today complain that the Muslim connection to the wall is only contrived to complicate negotiations over Jerusalem and legitimize Palestinian claims to the area. They observe that in earlier times, Muslims recognized the al-Aqsa Mosque as the holy site where Mohammed ascended to heaven. Muslims reply that what Jews call the Wailing Wall was never part of the original Second Temple, and they cite archeological evidence suggesting that the wall is only part of a retaining structure built to support the mount above. The response and reaction of both sides speak to the power of symbols, as well as to the notion that their meaning can be negotiated and changed over time.

This bin Laden tape shows the al Qaeda leader on a stallion. The horse and rider supply the visual cue, leading bin Laden's Middle Eastern audience to the subtextual message. Given his own rhetoric about the United States and Israel, there is little doubt that bin Laden means to suggest a connection to the symbolism of Mohammed and al-Barak, as well as reminding the audience about the Wall and Jerusalem.

❖ SUMMARY

In this chapter, we considered what mass media are and how entertainment media are different from news media. We also examined how broadcast media (television and radio) are different from print media (newspapers and magazines) and how public perceptions about terrorism are primed by representations of terrorists in entertainment media like popular cinema and genre literature. These allowed us to generalize about how terrorists and news media share in a symbiotic, mutually exploitative relationship. We also considered how public discourse about terrorism is primed by mediated stereotypical images of terrorists and terror violence and how these stereotypes are supported by mythology about terrorism, as well as by the news media's relationship with terrorism.

In the end, all of these factors regarding mass media combine with official rhetoric of our leaders, ideas about terror as rhetorical symbols, and the rhetorical choices that are made in defining an event as terrorism or an individual as terrorist. The combination allows us to see how terrorism truly is best understood as a communication process between terrorist and audience(s), the meaning for which is socially constructed in the public discourse and dialogue we have about the subject. Although this understanding may not shield us from the physical dangers of terror violence and destruction, it can help us to understand *why* we feel threatened by this violence and how it operates rhetorically. The violence of the tragedy on September 11 was visited physically only on those in New York, Washington, and Pennsylvania, but the psychological and emotional damage that came from the fear of these acts was shared by people in all corners of the world. Knowing how and why we feel threatened by what is, in the end, a communicative, rhetorical process is a starting place for considering how we should process the meaning of terrorism and, in the future, how we might respond.

## ❖ NOTES

1. Abraham H. Miller, *Terrorism, the Media and the Law* (New York: Transnational Publishers, 1982), p. 1.
2. Richard Campbell, *Media and Culture: An Introduction to Mass Communication* (New York: Bedford–St. Martin's Press, 2003), p. 6.
3. Ibid.
4. E.g., in the movie, a helicopter rescues three people from the sailboat *Mistral*, 50 miles off Long Island, but later has to ditch in the Atlantic when traveling to another rescue. In reality, it was a helicopter attempting to rescue a lone Japanese sailor 250 miles offshore that ditched when returning to the mainland.
5. E.g., demonstrators wishing to draw attention to animal rights and the fur trade might stage public relations events, such as a loud formal protest outside a department store hosting a fur fashion show, in the hope of drawing media attention. Make noise and possibly get arrested for disturbing the peace, and you have a better chance of drawing media coverage.
6. E.g., Howard Stern, who commands an audience in the millions for his syndicated radio program, also wrote two books, both of which were best-sellers based on his life. One of these books later became a movie—which did reasonably well at the box office and in video, starring Stern as himself. Though Stern is a funny writer and made a critically well-received acting

debut, there is no doubt that the appeal and success of his books and movie owed in no small measure to his built-in audience and already established status as a celebrity in radio.

7. Seth Mydans, "Researchers Put Together the Story of the Khmer Rouge," *New York Times*, September 15, 2002, p. 10.

8. E.g., Germany's radio broadcasts during the Second World War often employed British and American defectors such as William Joyce or Mildred Gillars (referred to as "Lord Hee Haw" and "Axis Sally") in an attempt to draw the sympathies of Britain and the United States to the Nazi cause—or, at the very least, to undermine the morale of British and American troops in the European theater. However, these radio broadcasts, operating in a larger marketplace of radio media, had to compete with many other programs and entertainment—ultimately unsuccessfully.

9. S. I. Hayakawa, *Language in Thought and Action*, 2d ed. (New York: Harcourt, Brace and World, 1964), p. 233.

10. E.g., early internal propaganda references to the party described communists as "peace loving, progressive and scientific," while describing outsiders as "war-mongering, bourgeois, reactionary, idealist and imperialist." Ibid., p. 236.

11. See, e.g., Elisabeth Rosenthal, "Beijing in a Rear-Guard Battle Against a Newly Spirited Press," *New York Times*, September 15, 2002, p. 1.

12. Joseph Conrad, *The Secret Agent*, rev. ed. (1907; New York: Oxford University Press, 1998).

13. Robert Louis Stevenson and Fanny van de Grift Stevenson, *The Dynamiter* (New York: Longmans Green, 1903).

14. Fyodor Dostoyevsky, *The Devils*, trans. David Magarshack (New York: Penguin Books, 1953); originally published as *Besy* (1871).

15. Liam O'Flaherty, *The Informer* (New York: Random House, 1925).

16. John LeCarré, *The Little Drummer Girl* (New York: Alfred A. Knopf, 1983).

17. I make this point based upon the gross number of books sold and their ultimate media convergence from books to screenplays for cinema or television. Of the authors mentioned, some (like Conrad) have had their works translated to the silver screen, and others (such as LeCarré) enjoy similar convergence and lasting commercial success today. These authors are, nevertheless, considered to have produced works of literature—which makes their work less appealing to a mass audience.

18. Thomas Harris, *Black Sunday* (1975; New York: E. P. Dutton, 2000).

19. William Granger, *November Man* (New York: Warner Books, 1993).

20. Tom Clancy, *Patriot Games* (New York: G. P. Putnam and Sons, 1987).

21. Tom Clancy, *Clear and Present Danger* (1989; New York: Berkeley Publishing Group, 1990).

22. See, e.g., Narmeen El-Farra, "Arabs and the Media," *Journal of Media Psychology* 1, no. 2 (1996): 1–7. El-Farra notes: "When it was released, this movie

created anger among Arab-Americans. The Arab community felt that the negative portrayal of Arabs, namely as terrorists, encouraged existing stereotypical views. Not only were the Arabs in the film religious fanatics bent on destroying the world, they were also sexist, racist and idiotic" (p. 4).

23. See, e.g., Jack Shaheen, *Reel Bad Arabs: How Hollywood Vilifies a People* (Northampton, MA: Interlink Books, 2001). In this work, Shaheen traces back some 1,000 films that stereotype Arabs as terrorists, oil-hoarding sheikhs, American-hating Muslim fanatics, brute murderers, sleazy fanatics, and abusers of women.

24. Perhaps this is intended as an homage (or more likely, a time-honored Hollywood tradition of plagiarism) to the real-life terrorist Carlos the Jackal.

25. If imitation is the sincerest form of flattery, this movie was amazingly flattered by the copycat films that followed, including 1992's *Under Siege* (*Die Hard* on a battleship), 1995's *Sudden Death* (*Die Hard* on the hockey rink), and 1997's *Air Force One* (*Die Hard* on the president's personal plane).

26. Jonathan Alter, "Jumping to Conclusions," *Newsweek*, May 1, 1995, p. 55.

27. El-Farra, "Arabs and the Media," p. 4.

28. Carlos, as quoted in John Follain, *Jackal: The Complete Story of the Legendary Terrorist, Carlos the Jackal* (New York: Arcade, 1998), p. 77.

29. Ibid., citing the memoirs of Iran's OEC Minister Jamshid Amouzegar. Amouzegar was one of the hostages taken by Carlos.

30. Frederick Forsyth, *The Day of the Jackal* (New York: Viking Press, 1971).

31. Robert Ludlum, *The Bourne Identity* (New York: Marek Books, 1980).

32. Robert Ludlum, *The Bourne Ultimatum* (New York: Random House, 1990).

33. M. Cherif Bassioni, "Terrorism and the Media," *Journal of Criminal Law and Criminology* 72 (1981): 1–55.

34. This was one of the ways CNN and later Al Jazeera television gained a competitive advantage over other networks.

35. Fouad Ajami, "What the Muslim World Is Watching," *New York Times Magazine*, November 18, 2001.

36. Mohammed El Nawaway and Adel Iskandar, *Al-Jazeera: How the Free Arab News Network Scooped the World and Changed the Middle East* (Cambridge, MA: Westview Press, 2002), p. 173.

37. Kathleen Hall Jamieson, *Dirty Politics: Deception, Distraction, and Democracy* (New York: Oxford University Press, 1992), p. 85.

38. See, e.g., Annemarie Schimmel, *And Muhammad Is the Messenger: The Veneration of the Prophet in Islamic Piety* (Chapel Hill: University of North Carolina Press, 1985), p. 159.

# Index

# About the Author

**Joseph S. Tuman** is Professor of Political and Legal Communications in the Department of Speech and Communication Studies at San Francisco State University. He is the recipient of the Jacobus tenBroek Society award for teaching excellence, and he has published widely in the field of political and legal communications, including the book *Freedom of Speech in the Marketplace of Ideas* (coauthored with Douglas Fraleigh), as well as numerous other international journal articles and book chapters. Professor Tuman has also taught at the University of California, St. Mary's College, the New School for Social Research, and Paris II, the top law school in France. His work has been featured in news publications including the *New York Times*, the *Los Angeles Times*, and the *San Francisco Chronicle*, and he has often contributed to local and national network news for ABC, NBC, CBS, CNN, and Fox News.